Violent criminal acts and actors

International Library of Sociology

Founded by Karl Mannheim

Editor: John Rex, University of Warwick

Arbor Scientiae
Arbor Vitae

A catalogue of the books available in the **International Library of Sociology** and other series of Social Science books published by Routledge & Kegan Paul will be found at the end of this volume.

olent criminal acts and actors

symbolic interactionist study

Lonnie H. Athens

Routledge & Kegan Paul
Boston, London and Henley

First published in 1980
by Routledge & Kegan Paul Ltd
39 Store Street, London WC1E 7DD,
Broadway House, Newtown Road,
Henley-on-Thames, Oxon RG9 1EN and
9 Park Street, Boston, Mas. 02108, USA
Photoset in 10 on 12 Times by
Kelly Typesetting Ltd, Bradford-on-Avon, Wiltshire
and printed in the United States of America by
Vail-Ballou Press Inc
© Routledge & Kegan Paul, 1980

British Library Cataloguing in Publication Data

Athens, Lonnie H.

Violent criminal acts and actors. –
(International library of sociology).
1. Offenses against the person
I. Title II. Series
364.1'5   HV6493   79–41011

ISBN 0 7100 0342 0

To my grandfather, L. D. Zaharias

Contents

Foreword

Sensitive and informed scholars of our contemporary social scene must be aware of the puzzling problem that is set by the occurrence and character of violent human conduct. On one hand, a growth in the extent and forms of violence seems to be taking place in conjunction with the increasing mobility of modern life. On the other hand, the steadily increasing scholarly study of violent behavior does not appear to yield much gain in the analysis and understanding of violent behavior. How is this to be explained? The lagging state of our scholarly knowledge of violent behavior is a reflection of the difficulties in isolating and studying the effective factors that are involved in violent behavior. We can appreciate this point more easily when we note that the areas in which we have succeeded in expanding our understanding represent areas or phases of violent behavior which carry some form of group endorsement or sanction. Thus, the violence that one notes today in guerrilla warfare, in political terrorism, or in gang warfare can be understood relatively easily when one considers the play of such justifying features as a sense of group mission or the feelings that are rooted in group affiliation. The genuine difficulties in analyzing and understanding violent behavior arise when one deals with violent behavior that lies outside of group endorsement and direction. Here, speaking metaphorically, violent conduct appears in a pristine form. It represents violent action that emerges outside of public sanction and in defiance of established laws and moral principles. It is the type of violent behavior which has challenged human societies since time immemorial. It is the type of violence that we are familiar with in the case of violent criminal offenders.

It may seem strange, indeed intemperate, to suggest that we are stymied in understanding violent criminal behavior. Few areas of human group life have been studied as assiduously as that of crime. The violent forms of criminal behavior, such as homicide, have been particularly the object of scientific study by many scholars over many decades. Such studies have yielded vast quantities of diversified data and have been attended by an abundance of theoretical schemes seeking to account for violent criminal behavior. Yet, I think that we must candidly admit that despite the vast amount of study and the many diverse directions of theorizing we have relatively little solid knowledge of violent criminal behavior. We get one indication of this in the confused and contradictory character of our theories and, indeed, of a great deal of our data. But more striking and important is the inability of our present criminological knowledge to offer a basis for genuinely effective control over violent criminal behavior, whether along the line of prevention or the line of correction. The record of efforts at control or elimination is dismal. We are forced to recognize that violent crime persists as a pressing and baffling problem even in our sophisticated and scientifically advanced societies.

Such an unfavorable observation immediately invites attention to the ways in which violent criminal behavior is being studied and analyzed. The failure to develop the desired body of scientific knowledge, despite the vast amount of serious study that has been undertaken, suggests that such study has not come to grips in a basic way with violent criminal behavior. It may be that a new approach is in order, one that comes closer to the detection and study of violent behavior as it actually takes place in the empirical world. This is essentially the lead that underlies the present work of Dr Lonnie Athens. He has sought in a pioneering effort to approach the study of violent criminal behavior from the point of view that has come to be known as 'symbolic interactionism.'

A brief explanation of symbolic interaction may be inserted here to help understand Dr Athens' line of study. The symbolic interactionist approach rests on the premise that human action takes place *always* in a situation that confronts the actor and that the actor acts on the basis of *defining this situation* that confronts him. Thus, the study of violent behavior would require that the student identify the way in which the actor sees and defines the situation in which he is placed and in which he comes to act violently. According to symbolic interactionism the observation of human behavior in this fashion brings one's study to the very threshold of the actual empirical behavior with which one is concerned. This approach to the study of violent action is definitely different from the outstanding conventional ways that mark the field of criminology. The conventional approaches to the study of violent crime lie predominantly along two lines: (a) to seek the causes or correlates of violent crime by pursuing aggregate studies and (b) to seek such causes in the personal make-up of the individual offender. The aggregate type of study rests on the premise that violent crime is to be understood by identifying the antecedent aggregate factors with which such crime is connected. The personality type of study favors a clinical probing into personality composition for factors to explain the violence. Neither of these two conventional approaches concerns itself first and foremost with the immediate violent act or with the experience of the violent offender in the formation and execution of his act. Instead, both approaches take the violent act as a 'given' without seeking to study it; they seek analysis and explanation by turning to 'causative' factors that are there prior to the violent act. Consequently, for both approaches the data and their explanation stand apart, remotely apart, from the violent act in its concreteness and its immediate happening. The conventional approaches jump away from an examination of the immediate empirical act that needs to be explained and they seek their data in areas long antecedent to and remote from the immediate empirical act. This is the reason why both of the conventional approaches fail in so many ways to explain criminal behavior, such as their inability to answer the following questions: (a) why do so many individuals not engage in violent behavior even though they have all of the characteristics of the aggregate population that is declared to have high causative or correlative relation with violent behavior; and (b) why does an offender with a constant personality make-up vary so pronouncedly in whether or not he engages in violent behavior even though his situations are objectively alike. It should be evident that the conventional study of criminal violence directs its attention elsewhere than to the action that constitutes the violence.

Dr Athens has focused his study on the violent acts of the offender. He has worked with a sizeable number of criminal violent offenders, studying them intensively. He has endeavored to have his informants describe their violent acts in a way that would allow him to identify their situations as seen by them and to trace their interpretation of these respective situations. This type of inquiry requires, admittedly, a great deal of skill and resourcefulness, such as an ability to establish good rapport with one's informants, to develop familiarity with their worlds, and to pursue flexible lines of questioning. Fortunately, Dr Athens is well qualified in all three respects. Through several years of experience he has come to know the world and the language of violent offenders, he is resourceful in establishing rapport with them, and he has developed a high order of skill in probing into their experiences. I know of no field sociologist who is better equipped than Dr Athens to pursue the type of inquiry described in this work.

Dr Athens' study of the violent action of criminals is to the best of my knowledge the only such study that has been made from the standpoint of symbolic interactionism. It is truly a pioneering effort and a rewarding effort. Without any previous study to chart the way, he has had to carve out his own scheme of analysis. In my judgment, he has done this in a very commendable fashion. He has identified the major ways by which his subjects defined the situations in which they committed their violent acts; this has enabled him to devise an intriguing classification of violent offenders. He has traced the general ways by which the process of interpretation furthers or inhibits violent action. He has shown, in the true spirit of George Herbert Mead, how the formation of self-images plays into and influences the interpretive process. And, using the knowledge derived from these lines of study, he has sought to distinguish between the different career lines of violent offenders – why some become fixed in violent behavior, why some become increasingly more violent, and why others steadily diminish their violence. All of these findings are of solid significance. They throw a great deal of light on matters that are either obscured or overlooked in conventional study. They suggest ways of exercising effective control of violent behavior. They point to lines of study that offer considerable promise of pinning down the elusive aspects of violent behavior. They make this book a very important book.

In my judgment, students in the social sciences in general and in criminology in particular will find the present work to be well worth their study and cogitation. It opens the door to a much-needed form of study in the grand task that confronts criminology.

HERBERT BLUMER
University of California
Berkeley, California

September 12, 1978

Acknowledgments

In conducting this study and preparing it for publication, I received the help of many persons. First, I would like to express my great debt to Herbert Blumer for his illumination of the nature of social action and the proper method for studying it. He also helped me in many significant ways with this research. He offered invaluable suggestions on how to improve the study as well as read and criticized several versions of the manuscript. Another person who deserves my special thanks is Marilyn O'Rourke Athens. She generously gave her time to this project and her suggestions were incorporated throughout the study. Without the help and encouragement of these two people, I could not have completed this book.

I am also very grateful to Sheldon Messinger. Besides pointing out to me the strengths and weaknesses of such a study, he critically read different versions of the manuscript. Jerome Skolnick is thanked for his ideas on how to write the methodological appendix and for first suggesting that I should try to publish this study as a book. For encouraging my early interest in criminology, I am indebted to Marshall Clinard.

I wish to express my appreciation for their co-operation to the staff members of the correctional institutions where I conducted this study. All the persons who participated in the study are also due a special word of thanks. Finally, I am indebted to the University of California-Berkeley for a Chancellor's Patent Fund Award which helped make this study possible.

LONNIE H. ATHENS

1 A review and critique of the dominant approaches taken in the study of violent criminality

The field of criminology has traditionally been divided into three major parts: criminalization, criminality, and corrections. Criminalization involves the study of the conditions under which the criminal laws develop and the process by which they are carried out. Criminality involves the study of criminal acts and/or the persons who commit them. Finally, corrections involves the study of the practices used to treat persons who have broken criminal laws. The present study falls into the second category. It focuses upon *violent criminality*, or more fully, the acts of criminal homicide, aggravated assault, and forcible rape, and the persons who commit them.

Over the last thirty years, three approaches have dominated the study of violent criminality: the external pattern approach, the personality approach, and the integrated approach.

External pattern approach

The external pattern approach is based upon the assumption that the discovery of empirical uniformities in the external characteristics, or 'material facts', of violent crimes will reveal their causes. Hypotheses that patterns exist in the characteristics of violent offenses, offenders and victims are implicitly or explicitly tested. In the studies done from this approach, usually the patterns of just one type of violent crime are studied. Thus, most of these studies are on the patterns of criminal homicide or aggravated assault or forcible rape, rather than on the patterns of violent crime in general.[1]

One of the best examples of this approach is provided by Pittman and Handy's study of aggravated assault in St Louis. According to

1

them, 'the purpose of this study is to analyze the crime of aggravated assault and to establish its "patterns" . . .' (1964: 462). For this purpose, they examined 241, or a 25 per cent random sample, of the 965 crimes classified as aggravated assault by the St Louis Metropolitan Police Department over a one-year period. Data were gathered from police reports filed on these crimes and from arrest records of the offenders and victims. Analyzing these data, Pittman and Handy tested hypotheses concerning such things as the time and location of the offense, the season of the year when they were committed, the type of weapons used by the offenders, the involvement of alcohol in the offense, the relationship of offenders to victims, and previous arrest records of offenders and victims.

Assuming that 'during weekdays interaction among people is limited by their work, and there is less leisure time than on the weekends,' Pittman and Handy hypothesized that 'the majority of the acts of aggravated assault would occur between 6.00 p.m. Friday and 6.00 a.m. Monday.' This hypothesis was confirmed, with 132 of the 241 offenses occurring during the stated time period. They further hypothesized that 'the majority of the acts would occur between 8.00 p.m. on a given evening and 4.00 a.m. the following morning.' This hypothesis was also confirmed, with 140 of the offenses occurring between 8.00 p.m. and 4.00 a.m. (1964: 463).

Pittman and Handy made several hypotheses about the location of the offenses and the season of year when they occurred. They first hypothesized that 'the largest number of acts would occur on public streets rather than in taverns or bars, residences or other places.' This hypothesis was confirmed with 110 of the 241 offenses taking place on public streets, 91 in residences, and only 27 in taverns or bars. With respect to season of the year, it was hypothesized that more acts would be committed during the winter than during other seasons. Since 87 of the offenses occurred during the summer months as compared to 82 during the winter months, this hypothesis was rejected. Considering the influence of the season of the year upon the location of the offense, they then hypothesized that 'during the winter months, a greater number of acts would occur indoors as against the summer, when the larger number would occur outdoors.' This hypothesis was also rejected since the number of offenses occurring indoors and outdoors was almost identical in the winter and in the summer (1964: 464).

With respect to the weapon used in the offense, Pittman and Handy hypothesized that 'a knife, being readily accessible, would

2

be used in more instances than any other weapon.' They found that a knife was used in 126 of the 241 cases, a gun in 39, and personal force in 14, thereby confirming the hypothesis. 'The fact that in Negro neighborhoods weapons for self defense are commonly carried' lead them to further hypothesize that 'proportionately, white offenders would use personal force to a greater extent than would Negro offenders.' This hypothesis was also confirmed with white offenders significantly more often than black offenders using personal force. Finally, they hypothesized that 'prior alcohol ingestion by both the offender and victim would be common in acts of aggravated assault.' This hypothesis was not confirmed, however. The ingestion of alcohol was found to be present in only slightly more than one-quarter of the cases (1964: 464–7).

Pittman and Handy tested several hypotheses under the heading of 'the relationship of offender and victim.' After finding that persons were of the same race in 228 cases and of the same sex in 144 cases, they reasoned that 'if the offender and victim were of the same race, they would be of the same sex.' This hypothesis was not supported by the data. Then on the assumption that 'persons of the same age are most likely to interact with one another,' they hypothesized that 'the victim and offender would be within the same age category.' This hypothesis was supported by the data with 146 of the 241 cases involving offenders falling within the same age groups (1964: 467).

The hypothesis that differences would be displayed in the prior arrest records of the offenders and victims was also tested. This hypothesis was confirmed. A significant difference was found in the frequency with which offenders and victims had previously been arrested. One hundred and fifty-six of the 248 offenders had prior arrest records, whereas only 121 of the 252 victims did. Thirty-seven of the offenders with prior records had been previously arrested at least once for assault. Lastly, it was hypothesized that 'Negro offenders would be no more likely to have prior arrest records than white offenders; this belief was confirmed' (1964: 468).

Pittman and Handy conclude from the analysis of these external characteristics that 'it is possible to state the expected pattern of aggravated assault in the "typical" case' (1964: 469). They describe the typical case in the following manner (1964: 469):

An act of aggravated assault is more likely to occur on a weekend than during the week, specifically between 6.00 p.m. Friday and

3

6.00 a.m. Monday. . . While the event shows little likelihood of being more frequent in the four summer months considered together than in the winter, this type of assault peaks in the months of July and August.

The crime will occur on a public street, or, secondly, in a residence. . .

The weapon used by both men and women will in most cases be a knife, with a gun the second choice. . .

These records indicate that neither the offender nor the victim will be under the influence of alcohol. . .

The offender and victim will be of the same race and of the same sex. . . Both will be of the same age group. . .

Negro offenders are no more likely than their white counterparts to have a prior arrest record. . .

Personality approach

The personality approach is based upon the assumption that pathological personality make-ups cause persons to commit violent crimes. Thus, hypotheses which link pathological or abnormal personalities to violent criminal behavior are implicitly or explicitly tested.[2] The most important example of this approach is provided by Megargee.

Megargee hypothesizes that a person who commits a violent crime almost always has one of two types of personalities. One type is called an undercontrolled personality and the other an over-controlled personality. Both are viewed as abnormal since they deviate from the normal personality in their level of self control or aggressive inhibitions. With respect to a person with an under-controlled personality, Megargee states (1966: 2):

> The Undercontrolled Aggressive person corresponds to the typical conception of an aggressive personality. . . He is a person whose inhibitions against aggressive behavior are quite low. Consequently, he usually responds with aggression whenever he is frustrated or provoked.

And with respect to a person with an overcontrolled personality, he states (1966: 2–3):

4

The Chronically Overcontrolled type behaves quite differently, however. His inhibitions against the expression of aggression are extremely rigid so he rarely, if ever, responds with aggression no matter how great the provocation. . . The result is that through some form of temporal summation. . . his instigation to aggression builds up over time. In some cases, the instigation to aggression summates to the point where it exceeds even his excessive defenses. If this occurs when there are sufficient cues to aggression in the environment, an aggressive act should result.

There is an important difference between the aggressive behavior of persons with under- and overcontrolled personalities. The difference lies in the nature of the relationship between: (1) the provocation or the immediate frustrating stimulus, (2) the instigation or drive to aggression, and (3) the resulting overt response. In the case of the undercontrolled person these are directly proportional to one another. The greater is the provocation, the stronger is the drive to aggression and the more aggressive is the overt response (1973: 39). But in the case of the overcontrolled person, these are usually disproportional to one another. Once his drive to aggression has summated or built up over time to a point which reaches his level of self control, the overcontrolled person makes an aggressive response of lethal intensity, even if he is only slightly provoked (1966: 22; 1973: 39). Thus, Megargee reasons that 'The former may commit aggressive responses of any intensity depending upon the immediate stimulus situation, while the latter tends to inhibit aggressive responses until they break through in . . . an extremely assaultive response in which the very life of the victim may be jeopardized' (1966: 17).

By way of analogy, Megargee describes persons with these two types of abnormal personalities (1965: 29):

Suppose we regard a man's inhibitions against aggression as a dam, and his impulses to aggression as the water which seeks to flow past. Whenever the water rises above the top of the dam, it spills over into the valley below, causing disturbance – but not nearly as much as if the dam suddenly collapsed in a rain storm and let go all at once.

The undercontrolled aggressive person . . . has inhibitions which are like a low or incomplete dam. Very little water is blocked, and very little backs up . . . Almost any provocation results in aggression, and the amount of aggression will be determined by the amount of provocation. . . The people downstream from him may, therefore, be in constant discomfort and apprehension and clamor for more protection.

The chronically overcontrolled type, however, is very different. His dam is both too high and too rigid. There is no 'water over the dam' which can be discharged and forgotten; no emergency bypasses or spillways. Not a drop gets through, and the people downstream are dry, and careless, and perhaps even contemptuous. The thought of disaster never occurs to them. But the pressure builds up and up, and must finally have a vent. Since the structure was not built to handle major strains, one drop too many may cause a complete rupture and release the pent-up fury all at once. And so explodes the unexpected crime of violence.

The most comprehensive study testing the under- and over-controlled personality hypothesis has been done by Megargee himself (1966). The rationale behind this study is that a sample of persons who have committed extremely assaultive acts should contain both over- and undercontrolled persons, while a sample of persons who have committed moderately assaultive acts should contain only undercontrolled persons. According to Megargee, 'On various indexes or measures of aggressiveness and control, then, the extremely assaultive group should appear less aggressive and more controlled *as a group* than would either the moderately aggressive group or a nonassaultive sample' (1966: 3).

Seventy-six male delinquents who were detained in a county juvenile hall for various offenses were selected as subjects. The subjects were divided into the following four groups: 9 boys who had committed extremely assaultive offenses (EA group), 21 boys who had committed moderately assaultive offenses (MA group), 20 boys who were detained only for incorrigibility (I group), and 26 boys who had committed property offenses only (PO group). The I and PO groups were matched with the assaultive groups on age, race, and number of prior detentions (1966: 6–7).

Data were collected on the subjects' predetention behavior, detention behavior, and personality make-ups. The data on pre-detention behavior were taken from probation officers' reports. Analysis of these data resulted in several findings. The more impor-tant ones include: (1) the EA group had significantly less previous detentions than did the MA group, (2) the EA group significantly more often had satisfactory school attendance records than did the other groups, and (3) the EA group more often, though not significantly, had satisfactory school conduct records than did the other groups (1966: 9–10).

Data on the behavior of the subjects during their detention in juvenile hall were obtained by means of an aggressive behavior checklist, a favorable behavior rating scale, and an overcontrolled behavior index derived from the Gough Adjective Checklist. Among the more important findings are: (1) the EA group had lower, though not significantly, verbal and physical aggression scores on the behavior checklist than did the other groups, (2) the EA group had a higher, but not significantly, score on the favorable behavior scale, than did the other groups, and (3) the EA group had a significantly higher score on the overcontrolled behavior index than did the other groups (1966–13).

Finally, the data on the personality make-ups of the subjects were provided by a battery of psychological tests: The California Personality Inventory (CPI), the Rosenzweig Picture-Frustration Test (P-F), the Thematic Apperception Test (TAT), and the Holtzman Inkblot Test (HIT). Among the more important findings which resulted from the analysis of these test data are: (1) the EA group had a higher, though not significantly, self control score on the CPI than did the other groups, (2) the EA group had a lower extrapunitive score on the P-F than did the MA group, but had a higher one than did the I or P groups, (3) the EA group displayed a lower need aggression score on the TAT than did the PO or I groups, but a higher one than the MA group, and (4) the EA group also displayed the highest hostility score on the HIT of all the groups (1966: 14–17).

Megargee concludes from his analysis of the predetention behavior, detention behavior, and personality make-ups of these four groups that 'the results were by no means unequivocal in their support for the hypothesis. Nevertheless, by and large, a review of the data indicates consistent if not spectacular support for the writer's hypothesis' (1966: 17–18). With respect to the generally negative findings produced by the psychological tests, he remarks that (1966: 17):

It is not too surprising that the behavior on the psychological tests is not as clear-cut as that observed in detention or found in the case history. Studies . . . have demonstrated the greater validity of case history as opposed to psychological tests. This tendency to find greater clarity in direct measures as opposed to tests would probably be accentuated in a correctional setting such as the one in which these data were collected.

Integrated approach

The integrated approach is based upon the assumption that a combination of social and psychological factors causes persons to commit violent crimes. These factors are, further, always assumed to be correlated. Thus, hypotheses about violent crime which link together both types of factors are formulated and tested. The best example of this approach to violent criminality is provided by Wolfgang and Ferracuti.[3]

Wolfgang and Ferracuti hypothesize that 'overt (and often illicit) expression of violence (of which homicide is only the most extreme) is part of a subcultural normative system and that this system is reflected in the psychological traits of the subcultural participants' (Ferracuti and Wolfgang, 1964: 294; Wolfgang and Ferracuti, 1967a:158). According to them, this subcultural normative system is localized within the lower social class of a society (Ferracuti and Wolfgang, 1963: 379–81; 1964: 293; Wolfgang, 1967: 11). To further fill out this hypothesis, they add seven corollary propositions (Ferracuti and Wolfgang, 1964: 294–8; Wolfgang and Ferracuti, 1967a: 158–61):

1   No subculture can be totally different from or totally in conflict with the society of which it is a part.
2   To establish the existence of a subculture of violence does not require that all persons sharing in this basic value element express violence in all situations.
3   The ubiquitous presence of potential resort to violence in a variety of situations emphasizes the penetrating and diffuse nature of this cultural theme.
4   The subcultural ethos of violence may be shared by all ages in a subsociety, but this ethos is most prominent in a limited age group ranging from late adolescence to middle age.
5   The counter-norm is non-violence.
6   The development of favorable attitudes toward, and the use of violence in this subculture usually involve learned behavior

and a process of differential learning, association or identification.

7 The use of violence in a subculture is not necessarily viewed as illicit behavior, and the users therefore do not have to deal with feelings of guilt about their aggression.

Wolfgang and Ferracuti qualify this hypothesis by making a distinction between 'idiopathic' and 'normatively prescribed' violent crimes. Idiopathic violent crimes are committed by persons who suffer from some major psychopathology, while normatively prescribed ones are committed by persons who are members of a subculture of violence. The former are usually from the middle or upper social classes and the latter are from the lower social class. The subculture of violence hypothesis does not, of course, apply to idiopathic violent crimes. Wolfgang and Ferracuti estimate that less than 10 per cent of the violent crimes committed are idiopathic and thereby imply that the application of the hypothesis to the problem of violent crime is limited very little (see Ferracuti and Wolfgang, 1964: 378, 381–2; Wolfgang, 1967: 6–7; Wolfgang and Ferracuti, 1967a: 140–1, 262–3; 1967b: 272–3).

The best known study testing the subculture of violence hypothesis is one conducted in Italy by Ferracuti, Lazzari, and Wolfgang (1970). The authors state that the purpose of the study is 'to examine the subculture of violence thesis as a possible explanation for the high rates of violent crimes in specific cultures and for the proneness towards the use of violence as a problem-solving mechanism' (1970: 87). Since Sardinia has a violent social code known as the 'vendetta barbaricina' as well as a higher rate of violent crime than other regions of Italy, the authors designed a study to compare Sardinian and non-Sardinian violent and non-violent offenders (1970: 10–11, 97). The rationale behind the study was that the Sardinian violent offenders should be members of a violent subculture and thus should be distinguishable from the other offenders in the ways prescribed by the subculture of violence hypothesis (1970: 87–8, 97).

Four groups of offenders comprised the subjects for the study: 30 violent and 26 non-violent offenders from Sardinia and 30 violent and 30 non-violent offenders from other regions of Italy. These offenders were selected from the records of an observation center where males between the ages of 18 and 25 are sent for clinical examination and penal classification. Data were drawn from the

9

offenders' files, which contained information on their offense and social and family backgrounds, and the results of psychological tests and a psychiatric examination given to them (1970: 98–9).

Although the analysis of these data resulted in numerous findings, only those which bear most directly upon the subculture of violence hypothesis will be described here. These findings resulted from the comparisons between the Sardinian and non-Sardinian violent offenders, and between the Sardinian violent and non-violent offenders. The most important findings resulting from the first comparison are: (1) The violent Sardinians committed cruel violent crimes significantly more often than did violent non-Sardinians (1970: 139). (2) The violent Sardinians committed violent crimes against family members significantly less often than did the violent non-Sardinians (1970: 142). (3) The violent Sardinians had significantly lower FC and significantly higher S scores on the Rorschach test than did violent non-Sardinians (1970: 144, 146). (4) Violent Sardinians, however, did not significantly differ in aggressive scores on the TAT or MAPS or Palo Alto Scale from violent non-Sardinians (1970: 108–9). (5) Finally, violent Sardinians less often – though not significantly – suffered from major psychiatric disturbances than did violent non-Sardinians (1970: 71).

The most important findings which resulted from the comparison between violent and non-violent Sardinian offenders are: (1) The violent Sardinians significantly more often had a lower educational level than did the non-violent Sardinians (1970: 127). (2) Violent Sardinians had significantly lower FC and significantly higher CF and S scores on the Rorschach test than did the non-violent Sardinians (1970: 144–6). (3) Violent Sardinians, however, did not differ significantly in aggressive scores on the TAT or MAPS or Palo Alto Scale from non-violent Sardinians (1970: 109). (4) Finally, the violent Sardinians significantly less often suffered from a major psychiatric disturbance than did non-violent Sardinians (1970: 71).

From these findings, Ferracuti, Lazzari and Wolfgang conclude that the Sardinian violent offenders are indeed different from the other offenders. 'Although these differences are not always clear-cut such as to allow a sharp differentiation or a predictability of violent behavior,' the authors state that 'they are all in the same theoretical direction and in agreement with the subculture of violence hypothesis' (1970: 109). The authors specifically point out here that the Sardinian violent offenders 'are more explosive, more hostile, and their crimes are committed with more cruelty' and that they less often exhibit psychopathology (1970: 109). But they do add with regard to their findings on the TAT, MAPS, and Palo Alto Scale that (1970: 110):

> The failure of the psychological tests to differentiate our groups both in thematic data and in the Palo Alto Scale is not entirely unexpected. . . . Other tests . . . might yield other results, but the semantics of violence, as expressed in phantasy themes, and other cultural variants may render cross-cultural use difficult or impossible.

Critique of the dominant approaches

The three approaches just illustrated, like most approaches taken in the study of criminality, are based upon positivism (see Jeffery, 1960; Matza, 1964: 1–32; Vold, 1958: 27–40; Taylor *et al.*, 1973: 1–66). Positivism is the application of the logic of the physical sciences to the social and psychological sciences. The fundamental assumption of positivistic approaches is that human action is determined or caused by certain identifiable antecedent factors whose operation does *not* depend upon their playing a part in the interpretations which persons make when they act. As a result, the study of human action is reduced to the empirical examination of antecedent factors, or their indicators and correlates, and behavior, i.e., overt conduct.

It can easily be seen that the dominant approaches taken in the study of violent criminality are positivistic. In the case of the external pattern approach, the assumption is that the antecedent factors which cause violent criminal behavior will be indicated by the study of the patterns in the external characteristics of violent offenses, offenders, and victims. Thus, only findings on the superficial derivatives of violent criminality are provided. In the personality approach, the assumption is that the antecedent factor is an abnormal personality, and thus only findings on the personality make-ups of violent offenders or their correlates are provided. Finally, in the integrated approach, the assumption is that the antecedent factors are both social and psychological. Thus, only findings on the social and psychological characteristics of violent offenders are provided.

But positivistic approaches have two serious shortcomings. First, they ignore the fact that human action is *situated*: it always takes place within a context or situation which must be *interpreted* by the person who is confronted with the situation (see Deutscher, 1970). Blumer refers to this fact in his identification of two primary conditions of human action (1962: 187):

> One primary condition is that action takes place in and with regard to a situation. . . . any particular action is formed in the light of the situation in which it takes place. This leads to the recognition of a second major condition, namely, that the action is formed or constructed by interpreting the situation. The acting unit necessarily has to identify the things which it has to take into account – tasks, opportunities, obstacles, means, demands, discomforts, dangers, and the like; it has to assess them in some fashion and it has to make decisions on the basis of the assessment.

In other words, a human being constructs or forms his action *vis-à-vis* a situation. He interprets a situation by defining what confronts him and judging how he should handle it. On the basis of his interpretation, he carries out his own line of action in the situation.

To say that human action is situated does not, however, imply that antecedent factors play no role in human action. In so far as they enter into a person's interpretation of a situation, antecedent factors play a significant role in his action. But the study of antecedent factors or their indicators or correlates *cannot* be substituted for the study of the interpretations in which they are presumed to operate; their role in the interpretation of situations can only be ascertained through the study of that process. The nature of the interpretations of the situation through which some given type of human action is constructed cannot be taken for granted. Since interpretations of the situation are a *creative or formative process in their own right* rather than simply a product of antecedent factors, they must always be made a special object of analysis in the study of human action. Blumer makes this point below (1969: 16):

> We must recognize that the activity of human beings consists of meeting a flow of situations in which they have to act and that their action is built on the basis of what they note, how they assess . . . what they note, and what kind of projected lines of action they map out. This process is not caught by ascribing

action to some kind of factor (for example, motives, need-dispositions, role requirements, social expectations, or social rules) that is thought to initiate the action and propel it to its conclusion; such a factor, or some expression of it, is a matter the human actor takes into account in mapping his line of action. The initiating factor does not embrace or explain how it and other matters are taken into account in the situation that calls for action. One has to get inside of the defining process of the actor in order to understand his action.

A second shortcoming of positivistic approaches follows from the first one. In assuming that human action is determined primarily by antecedent factors, the human being is treated as merely a neutral medium through which given antecedent factors come to expression. Positivistic approaches thereby operate upon a model of the human being which views him as a *passive agent* who plays no role or part in the formation of his actions. But a human being constructs or forms his action through an interpretative process which, as just noted, is not determined solely by antecedent factors. Thus, the proper model of the human being is one which views him as an *acting unit* or *actor* who organizes his actions to fit the situations that confront him. With respect to these two different models of the human being, Blumer states (1969: 14):

> The dominant prevailing view sees the human being as a complex organism whose behavior is a response to factors playing on the organization of the organism. Schools of thought in the social and psychological sciences differ enormously in which of such factors they regard as significant, as is shown in such a diverse array as stimuli, organic drives, need-dispositions, conscious motives, unconscious motives, emotions, attitudes, ideas, cultural prescriptions, norms, values, status demands, social roles, reference group affiliations, and institutional pressures. . . . Nevertheless, these schools of thought are alike in seeing the human being as a responding organism, with its behavior being a product of the factors playing on its organization or an expression of the interplay of parts of its organization.

But he adds that the human being is (1969: 15)

> not a mere responding organism but an acting organism – an organism that has to mold a line of action on the basis of what it

13

takes into account instead of merely releasing a response to the play of some factor on its organization.

Positivistic approaches by their very design, however, are unable to take into account the fact that human action is situated and human beings are acting units (see Blumer, 1969: 55–7, 132–9). As noted, in these approaches the study of human action is reduced to the empirical examination of antecedent factors or their indicators or correlates and their end product—overt conduct. The interpretation made by a person of a situation in which he performs some action is left totally unexamined, and as a result, the role that he plays in the organization of his action is completely omitted. Thus, no empirical findings are provided on the process by which a person interprets a situation as calling for a certain line of action and then carries out this line of action. Yet without detailed knowledge of this process, human action cannot be adequately explained.

Given the limitations of positivistic approaches, a different type of approach needs to be taken in the study of human action. What is needed is an *interpretative* approach, that is, an approach which is based upon the recognition that human action is *situated* and which operates upon a model of the human being as an *actor*.[4] The primary requirement of such an approach is that the viewpoint of the person whose actions are under study always be explicitly taken into account in explaining his conduct (see Cooley, 1926; Schutz, 1954; Winch, 1958; Znaniecki, 1968: 34–89). Blumer states the necessity for doing this as follows (1969: 73–4):

> Since action is forged by the actor out of what he perceives, interprets, and judges, one would have to see the operating situation as the actor sees it, perceive objects as the actor perceives them, ascertain their meaning in terms of the meaning they have for the actor, and follow the actor's line of conduct as the actor organizes it – in short, one would have to take the role of the actor and see his world from his standpoint.

The purpose of the study that follows is to take an interpretative approach to the problem of violent criminality. The nature of the specific interpretative approach which will be taken is described in the next chapter.

2 Symbolic interactionism: an interpretative approach

The foundations of symbolic interactionism, an interpretative approach for the study of human action, are laid out by George Herbert Mead (1964, 1938, 1936, 1934, 1932) and Herbert Blumer (1975, 1969, 1962, 1937). The frame of reference used in the present study is derived primarily from the works of these two men.

Frame of reference

The central concept of symbolic interactionism is the self (Blumer, 1962: 181). The self has two basic aspects – the self as *process* and as *object*. The first aspect, the self as process, refers to the fact that a human being interacts with himself.[1] He carries on this self inter-action by making indications to himself and then responding to these indications by making further self indications. Self indications are made by an actor whenever he notes or points out something to himself.

The process of making self indications has two essential features. (1) The actor makes these indications to himself *as if* he were making them to someone else, except that he makes them in a *shorthand* or more abbreviated and rapid manner. (2) When making self indications, an actor is always role taking or implicitly indicating something to himself from the standpoint of another person, a small discrete group of persons, or a generalized other.

By interacting with himself in this way, the actor constructs interpretations of the situations which confront him. Interpret-ations of the situation have two on-going and correlated phases. The first phase is *definition*. Here the actor defines the nature of the

15

situation facing him. He does this by taking the role or roles of the other persons in the situation and indicating to himself from their standpoints the character of the gestures which they are making. Thus, the situation is defined by the actor primarily in terms of what he sees is being done and is likely to be done by the other participants in the situation.

The second phase in interpreting the situation is *judgment*. Here the actor decides upon the proper course of action to take in the situation, given his definition of it. He judges the situation by taking the role of a *generalized other* and indicating to himself from that standpoint how he ought to act. The role of a generalized other is the perspective of an abstract other or group which the actor himself carves out over time from his interaction with other persons. The role of the *particular* generalized other that he takes in judging a situation depends upon his definition of the situation. By taking the role of a generalized other, the actor forms a 'plan of action' to carry out in the situation; that is, he covertly organizes or prepares himself to follow a particular course of overt action.

But after the actor has judged the situation before him, he still may not carry out the resultant plan of action. He can always *redefine* the situation confronting him before carrying out this plan, if, for example, he notes that the other participants have altered their previous lines of action. If the actor forms a new definition of the situation, then he may *rejudge* it by again taking the role of a generalized other and indicating to himself how he should *now* respond to the situation. As a result, he may form a *new* plan of action. Thus, once formed, a plan of action can always be dropped and replaced by another (Blumer, 1969: 55, 73, 96).

The second aspect of the self, the self as object, refers to the fact that a human being has a conception or picture of himself which is his *self image*. An actor develops a self image by looking at himself and then judging what he sees. He can neither directly see nor judge himself but can only indirectly do so from a standpoint outside of himself. The only way that an actor can see and judge himself from the outside is by taking the roles of others and addressing himself from their standpoints. First he takes the roles of selected persons, such as his spouse or best friend, and small discrete groups, such as his family or gang, and looks at himself from their standpoints. The views that they hold of him are based upon how they interpret his actions, so that to them 'he is how he acts.' The actor then takes the roles of his generalized others and from these standpoints judges the particular ways in which such persons and groups view him. By judging their views of him from the roles of his generalized others, he forms an image of himself as this or that kind of person (see Mead, 1934: 138, 309; Blumer, 1969: 12–13).

The self as process and object are linked together by the generalized others of the actor. They enter into both his interpretations of situations and his self image. The actor judges the situations which confront him as well as the views that others have of him from the standpoints of his generalized others.[2] Thus, the image that he holds of himself is generally in line with the interpretations of situations that he forms. His generalized others may, of course, change over time. As they change, he will begin to judge both situations and himself differently, then engage in new forms of conduct, and eventually develop a new self image.

Description of the study

In the study that follows the frame of reference just described is applied to the problem of violent criminality. Thus, data were collected and analyzed on the interpretations violent actors make of violent situations, the self images they hold, as well as their violent careers.

I gathered data on these three topics primarily by conducting private, informal, and in-depth interviews with fifty-eight offenders convicted of criminal homicide, aggravated assault, forcible and attempted forcible rape, and robbery where the victim was seriously injured. Forty-seven of the offenders interviewed were men and eleven were women. Their ages ranged from mid-teens to late forties. A more complete description of them in terms of their offense, sex, and approximate age is presented at the end of Appendix A.

At the time of the interviews, twenty-three of the offenders were inmates of a prison in a midwestern state[3] and the remaining thirty-five were inmates of a jail or prison in a far western state. The way in which I selected the inmates for interviews, conducted my interviews with them, and validated the information they provided me is also discussed in Appendix A. In addition, my participant-observation of violent actors and acts was drawn upon in the study. This is described in Appendix B.

Finally, all fifty-eight persons whose interviews were used in the analysis which follows committed some type of *substantial* violent

17

criminal act; that is, the victim was either (1) substantially physically injured, i.e., non-accidentally injured either fatally or to a degree that usually calls for a physician's attention, such as results from a shooting, stabbing, clubbing, or relentless beating; or (2) substantially sexually violated, as in the case of coitus, sodomy, fellatio, or cunnilingus, either under the threat of the infliction of substantial physical injury or the actual infliction of substantial or less severe physical injury. Thus, the present study only applies to *substantial* violent criminal acts and those who commit them.

3 Self as process: interpretation of the situation

Data were gathered on the self processes of the fifty-eight offenders by having them describe in a detailed fashion what happened during the situations in which they committed their violent crimes and what, if anything, went through their minds as these situations unfolded. The study of these data shows two things. First, it suggests that violent actors *do* form interpretations of the situations in which they commit violent criminal acts. Further, the interpretations that they form of these situations account for their violent actions. In all of the cases the actors did at least two things. (1) By taking the roles of their victims they implicitly or explicitly indicated to themselves the character of the victim's gestures. (2) By taking the role of a generalized other, they implicitly or explicitly indicated to themselves that they *ought* to respond violently. Thus, the data show that violent actors *self consciously construct* violent plans of action before they commit violent criminal acts, as the examples which will appear shortly demonstrate.

This empirical finding almost completely contradicts the previous literature on this issue. With only one exception (Hartung, 1966: 136–54), psychiatrists, psychologists and sociologists have argued that most violent criminal acts are committed as a result of *unconscious* motivations, *deep* emotional needs, *inner* psychic conflicts, or sudden *unconscious* emotional bursts. For example, Banay, a psychiatrist, asserts that 'the true nature of the psychological phenomena of violence which causes one human being to inflict death upon another will remain shrouded in mystery unless a detailed psychiatric study traces down the inner motivations' (1952: 33). Similarly, Abrahamsen states that 'It is safe to say that

19

unconscious elements play an overwhelming part in homicide, and if uncovered, they will provide us with material enabling us to establish the dynamic connection between the killer's mind and his homicide' (1960: 196). Tanay, another psychiatrist, asserts that 'ego-dystonic homicide describes a killing that occurs against the conscious wishes of the perpetrator,' and he later adds that 'the majority of homicides are ego-dystonic' (1972: 815, 817). Further, on the basis of their review of the literature on 'murderers and murders,' the Lesters, two psychologists, state (1975: 5):

> Real murderers are not usually motivated by any long-range plans or conscious desires. Most commonly, they kill during some trivial quarrel, or their acts are triggered by some apparently unimportant incident, while deep and unconscious emotional needs are their basic motivation. Most murders occur on sudden impulse and in the heat of passion, in situations where the killer's emotions overcome his ability to reason.

Finally, in their joint works, Wolfgang, a sociologist, and Ferracuti, a psychologist, contend that 90 per cent of criminal homicides are 'passion crimes' (1967a: 140–1; 1967b: 272–3) which 'are unplanned, explosive, determined by sudden motivational bursts' (1967a: 209). They add that in such aggressive crimes the offender acts 'quickly' so that 'neither reasoning nor time for it are at his disposal' (1967a: 263).

The second thing that the study of these data suggests is that the 'interpretations of situations' in which violent criminal acts are committed fall into four distinct types. The following discussion of each of these types of interpretations of situations should make clearer how the interpretive process works in violent criminal acts. The first type of interpretation is termed 'physically defensive'.

Physically defensive

There are two essential steps in the formation of physically defensive interpretations of the situation. First, by taking the role of the victim, the actor implicitly or explicitly indicates to himself that the meaning of the victim's gestures is either (1) that the victim will very shortly physically attack him or an intimate such as a spouse or child or (2) that the victim is already physically attacking him or an intimate. Secondly, by taking the role of a generalized other, the actor then implicitly or explicitly indicates to himself that he ought to respond violently toward the victim and calls out within himself a violent plan of action. The meaning to the actor of his violent plan of action is that it is the only means of preventing another person from inflicting physical injury upon him or an intimate. The key feature of all physically defensive interpretations is that a gesture is made by the victim that the actor designates to himself as foreshadowing a physical attack or as directly indicating that a physical attack is taking place. Case 18 illustrates the nature of physically defensive interpretations of the situation.

Case 18 (criminal homicide)

'I was sitting at a bar drinking a beer when this guy sitting next to me went to play the pinball machine. When he came back to the bar, he said "You've been drinking my beer. I had a full can of beer when I went over to play that pinball machine." I said, "I ain't drank none of your beer." He said, "You better buy me another can of beer." I said, "Shit no, I ain't." At first I didn't know whether he really thought I had drank some of his beer or was just trying to bluff me into buying him a can, but when he later said, "You're gonna buy me another fucking can of beer," I knew then he was handing me that to start some crap so I knew for sure that I wasn't gonna buy him any beer. He told me again to buy him a beer. I said, "Hell, no." I figured if I showed him that I wasn't gonna buy him a beer he wouldn't push it, but he said, "You better go on and buy me another fucking beer." All I said then was, "I don't want any trouble; I'm just out of the pen, so go on and leave me alone cause I ain't about to buy you any beer." He just kept looking. Then I started thinking he was out to do something to me. He pulled out a knife and made for me, and I shot him once in the arm. He kept on coming so I had to finish him off. He was out to kill me.'

Further, when an actor injures or kills another person as a result of forming a physically defensive interpretation, his violent criminal act is *victim-precipitated*. This conceptualization of victim precipitation is *not* reducible to the externally based one put forth by Wolfgang. Wolfgang conceives of victim precipitation with respect to criminal homicide where 'the role of the victim is characterized by his having been the first in the homicide drama to use physical force directed against his subsequent slayer. The victim-precipitated cases are those in which the victim was the first to show

21

and use a deadly weapon, to strike a blow in an altercation – in short, the first to commence the interplay or resort to physical violence' (1957: 2). In a later paper, he explicitly states that the criteria which he used 'to classify . . . victims as precipitators of their own deaths were based on overt physical behavior' and that 'words alone were not enough' (1969: 72). Thus, a violent criminal act could be: (1) victim-precipitated according to Wolfgang's conception and follow from a physically defensive interpretation, that is, the victim makes the first overt violent response and is later slain, but he does so after indicating to himself that the offender's gestures indicate that a physical attack upon him or an intimate is imminent and through further self indication judges that a violent response is the means of preventing the offender from inflicting injury upon him or them; (2) victim-precipitated according to Wolfgang's conception but not follow from a physically defensive interpretation, that is, the victim makes the first violent response and is later slain, but does not do so upon the judgment that a violent response is the means of preventing the offender from inflicting injury upon him or an intimate, and (3) non-victim-precipitated according to Wolfgang's conception but follow from a physically defensive interpretation, that is, the actor does not make the first overt violent response but responds violently after indicating to himself that the other's physical attack upon him or an intimate is occurring, and through further self indication judges a violent response to be the best means of meeting the other's violent response. The relationship between these two ways of conceptualizing victim precipitation just described not only makes it clear that the two are not congruent with one another, but also directs attention to the fundamental problem with the behavioristic conceptualization of victim precipitation advanced by Wolfgang. It leads to the inclusion of many cases in which the victim *is not* a genuine contributing factor in the offense and leaves out as well many cases in which the victim *is* a genuine contributing factor in the offense.

Frustrative

The second type of interpretation of the situation in which violent criminal acts are committed is termed 'frustrative.' Frustrative interpretations of the situation are formed in two basic steps. First, by taking the role of the victim, the actor implicitly or explicitly indicates to himself that the meaning of the victim's gestures is

22

either (1) that the victim is resisting or will resist the *specific* line of action that the actor seeks to carry out or (2) that the actor should co-operate in a *specific* line of action that he does not want carried out. Secondly, by taking the role of a generalized other the actor then implicitly or explicitly indicates to himself that he ought to respond violently toward the victim and calls out within himself a violent plan of action. The meaning to the actor of his violent plan of action is that physical violence is the most appropriate means of handling another person's potential or attempted blockage of the larger act that the actor wants to carry out—for example, robbery, sexual intercourse, car theft – or a means to block the larger act that the other person wants to carry out – for example, calling the police or arrest. The mark of all frustrative interpretations is that the actor designates to himself the direction along which the larger act is heading and his desire for the act not to follow that course. Cases 49 and 10 illustrate the two ways that actors form frustrative inter-pretations.

Case 49 (forcible rape)

'I was listening to the radio in my apartment when I got horny and started thinking about getting me some pussy. I thought that I'd go down to the—district and find a nice white broad to bust my nut in. I knew the area pretty good, and it was far enough away from my own house. So I went out and jumped the—bus. I rode it to—street and then got off and started walking around. I got a good look at this middle-aged white broad walking around some apartments, and I said to myself, "I'm going to get that pussy and enjoy it."

'I followed her up to the entrance of an apartment building. She used a key to get into the main door, and I had to get to it fast before it shut. I barely got to the door in time, but I waited a few seconds before I walked in since I didn't want her to see me. When I went in, I heard her going up the stairs and I followed her. As soon as I got to the top of the stairs, I spotted her walking down the hallway, and I crept up behind her. When she opened the door to her apartment, I put my hands over her mouth, pushed her through the door and said, "Don't make a sound." Then I shut the door behind me and said, "If you make one fucking sound, I'll kill your ass."

'I didn't want her to panic too soon, so I threw her off base and said, "Do you have any money?" She said, "All I have is the $10 in my church envelope." I said, "Well, give it here." She took the

23

envelope out of her purse and handed it to me. Then I said, "Take your coat off." I took a long look at her and thought, "I'm going to drive this broad all night long."

'I grabbed her by the shoulders and threw her to the floor. She started yelling, "What are you doing, what are you doing?" I figured that I better let her know that I meant business, so I jumped right on her ass and started smashing her in the face and saying, "Shut up, shut up." As soon as she did, I stopped hitting her. Then I pulled her dress up above her waist and reached for her meat, and she started screaming "Stop, stop, stop" and stomped the floor with her feet. I just thought, "I have got to shut her ass up fast before somebody hears her," and then I really cut loose on her with lefts and rights and said, "Shut up, shut up, before I beat you to death." Finally she shut the fuck up, and I pulled her dress back up, tore her panties off her legs and . . .'

Case 10 (criminal homicide)

'I was low on cash and had heard about a good place to make a hit. About an hour later, my friend and I were punching the safe when a real young cop came in with his gun drawn and said, "You're under arrest; put your hands up." The first thing I thought was here is ten years and I don't want to do any more fucking time. I decided then that I wasn't going to give myself up. The cop walked up closer to us and I thought about getting his gun away from him, but I wondered where his partner was. He looked nervous, scared. I thought in the back of my mind that he would not use the gun, but I didn't care either. Then I figured he didn't have any partner and about hitting him. I had to get out of the situation. When he got right up to us, I hit him with the hammer.'

Malefic

The third type of interpretation of the situation in which violent criminal acts are committed is termed 'malefic.' Malefic interpretations are formed in a three-step process. First, by taking the role of the victim, the actor implicitly or explicitly indicates to himself that the meaning of the victim's gestures is that he is deriding or badly belittling the actor. Secondly, by taking the role of a generalized other, the actor implicitly or explicitly indicates to himself that the victim is an extremely evil or malicious person. Finally, by making further self indications from the role of a generalized other, the actor implicitly or explicitly indicates to himself that he ought to respond violently toward the victim and calls out within himself a violent plan of action. The meaning to the actor of his violent plan of action is that physical violence is the most fitting way of handling evil or malicious persons who make derogatory gestures. The key feature of all malefic interpretations is that the actor judges the victim to be extremely evil or malicious. Case 35 illustrates how an actor forms a malefic interpretation.

Case 35 (aggravated assault)

'I was just cruising around with some friends of mine drinking wine, smoking dope, and eating a few reds. We came to an intersection and slowed down to make a turn when this black dude in a Thunderbird coming the other way cut us off in the middle of the intersection while he made a turn. Then he drove by us with a big grin on his face throwing the bone. The friend of mine who was driving just turned and started going the other way, but I suddenly said to myself "that dirty jive nigger flipping me off and grinning—now he thinks he's one bad nigger; well, I'm going to get down with that black motherfucker." Then I grabbed the wheel and said, "Turn around and catch that nigger driving that Thunderbird." We started following him, but after he made a couple of turns, we lost him. He was too far ahead of us. I said "Well, he's got to be somewhere in this neighborhood, so let's just keep driving around here until we spot that Thunderbird, because I'm out to book that nigger." I could still see his big grin when he shot us the bird, and it was driving me up a wall. There was just no way that I was going to quit looking for that motherfucker. I was outright determined to have his ass one way or another.

'Finally I spotted his car in a driveway in front of a house, and I told X who was driving to pull over and park in front of the house. Then I snapped my shotgun together and loaded it. One of my friends said, "Hey, Y, what the hell is your trip?" I said, "It's just my trip" and jumped out of the car. I didn't care about anything but having that nigger's ass. All I thought was, "I'm going to kill this punk." I walked up to the house and knocked on the front door. He answered the door, but as soon as he saw it was me, he slammed it shut in my face. Then I kicked the door wide open and saw him making tracks out the back door. I ran through the house after him and jammed him as he was climbing over the back fence. I leveled the barrel of my shotgun at his head and said, "Nigger, get off that fence." After he did, I said, "Head back into that house." I wanted to fuck him up in the house so nobody would see it, but when we got to the back door, he stopped and said, "Man, I haven't done anything to you, please don't hurt me." His sniveling made me madder. I shoved the barrel into his back and said, "Man, go into that house." He still wouldn't go in, but just kept begging me not to shoot him. This pissed me off even more. I lost all my patience and said "Fuck it" and shot him right where he was standing.'

Frustrative-malefic

The final type of interpretation of the situation in which violent criminal acts are committed is termed 'frustrative-malefic' since it combines features of the prior two types. Frustrative-malefic interpretations are formed in a three-step process. First, by taking the role of the victim the actor implicitly or explicitly indicates to himself that the meaning of the victim's gestures is either that he is resisting some *specific* line of action that the actor wants to carry out or that he wants the actor to co-operate in some *specific* line of action that the actor does not want carried out. Secondly, by taking the role of a generalized other, the actor implicitly or explicitly indicates to himself that the victim's gestures are irksome or malicious and consequently, the victim is evil or malicious. Finally, by making further self indications from the role of a generalized other, the actor implicitly or explicitly indicates to himself that he ought to respond violently toward the victim and calls out within himself a violent plan of action. The meaning to the actor of his violent plan of action is that physical violence is the most appropriate way to deal with the potential or attempted blockage by an evil or malicious person of the larger act that he seeks to carry out or the most appropriate way to block the larger act that an evil or malicious person wants to carry out. The mark of all frustrative-malefic interpretations is that they always start out as frustrative interpretations but then switch into malefic interpretations before the actor makes his violent response. Case 21 illustrates the nature of frustrative-malefic interpretations of the situation.

Case 21 (aggravated assault)

'I was at a neighborhood tavern drinking beer next to this guy who I knew was a homosexual. He was showing his billfold around and I began to think about hustling him. We were in the bathroom together several times and I tried to hustle him, but he acted sneaky [he didn't put up any money], so I punched him. He then left the tavern threatening to call the police on me. I thought that mother-fucking queer, I should rob him and bust his fucking head. So I followed him. He went home. I knocked on his door, but he wouldn't answer. I got mad and kicked his door open. Then this guy, his boyfriend, who was shacking up with him, comes up to me. His boyfriend being there got me madder, so I punched the boyfriend. The boyfriend took off out the front door. I then caught that queer standing there watching and staring at me. This got me madder. I figured this was a good opportunity to rob him and mess him up too. I've gone this far, so I might as well go all the way and do a good job on him. I'm in trouble as it is. You can get just as much time for doing a good job as a bad one. I wanted to fuck him up. I started beating him.'

4   When interpretations of the situation lead to violent criminal acts

The data on the interpretations of situations just described pertain only to situations in which the actors actually committed a violent criminal act; that is, they were *completed* violent situations. In other words, these data were gathered in a retrospective fashion starting from the fact that an overt violent act was committed, rather than starting from the covert process of interpretation that preceded it. Thus, the conclusion which can be drawn from this is that whenever a violent criminal (i.e., substantial violent) act has been committed, one of the interpretations posited – physically defensive, frustrative, malefic, or frustrative-malefic – was necessarily at play. This, however, leaves open the question of whether a violent criminal act is committed every time one of these interpretations is formed.

But this question can be addressed with the help of data gathered on interpretations made by offenders of situations in which they *almost*, but did *not*, actually commit a violent criminal act, that is, of *near* violent situations. This was done by having them describe in a detailed fashion what, if anything, they indicated to themselves, and how, if at all, they judged these self indications during situations in which they almost committed violent criminal acts. The study of these materials shows that the interpretations of near violent situations fall into the same four types already described for completed violent situations. Then the interpretations of completed violent and near violent situations of the same type were compared. For example, malefic interpretations which were formed in completed violent situations were compared with those which were formed in near violent situations, etc.

These comparisons of interpretations formed in completed

violent and in near violent situations suggest that the occurrence or non-occurrence of three possible events determines whether or not a violent criminal act is committed. The first event is termed a 'fixed line of indication.'

Fixed line of indication

A fixed line of indication occurs when the actor continues to call out within himself a violent plan of action until he overtly responds violently. After once forming one of the violent interpretations, he fails to consider anything else in the situation besides acting violently. He either immediately carries out his violent plan of action in overt conduct or he further nurtures it along by continuing to indicate to himself from the role of a generalized other that he ought to respond violently until he finally does carry out the plan of action into overt conduct. Case 33 below illustrates an actor who formed a malefic interpretation and then stayed in a fixed line of indication.[1]

Case 33 (aggravated assault)

'I was over at my partner's pad drinking wine and smoking dope late one night, and I called a taxi to take me home since I had wrecked my car. The driver pulled up, and I ran out. I opened the door to his taxi, and he asked me where I was going. I told him to—street in—, and he said, "Well, that's over a ten mile trip; you'll have to pay me the fare in advance before I'll drive you there." I got mad as shit because I wanted to get home, and I didn't have any cash to be paying him in advance with. I said, "You're fucking crazy, old man; I've taken a taxi there many times at night and never had to pay in advance; my dad will pay you your money as soon as we get there; here's my wallet, you can look at my name." He said, "All right, get in; don't get shook up, I believe you; I don't need to see your wallet."

'As soon as we took off, he started telling me about all the times that he had been burnt by people taking his cab. I just said to myself, "Why is this old bastard telling me all this shit? I'm not going to rip him off; I told him that I was going to pay him." I just sat in the back of the taxi not saying a word, and he kept on telling me about how people were always ripping him off, along with all the other problems that he had. I thought, "Man, I've got five times as many troubles as he has; he must really be a weak person to be telling someone that he doesn't even know all about his personal problems. I don't want to hear this bullshit." Finally his crying to me set my blood boiling. The old fucker was really irking me.

'When he drove the taxi down the street that my house was on, I said to myself, "This old motherfucker handed me all that shit before I could even get in his taxi, and he has been sniveling to me the whole fucking time I've been riding in it. Fucking s.o.b., I'm going to cut his stinking throat." As soon as he stopped the cab, I opened up my knife and put the blade to him.'

Case 37 illustrates an actor who formed a physically defensive interpretation and then stayed in a fixed line of indication.

Case 37 (criminal homicide)

'I was over at my friend's place just sitting around drinking whiskey with him and another guy. This other dude then came over, and we began shooting dice for half dollars. After about an hour or so of shooting dice, I started feeling the whiskey and decided that I better be leaving. I told them that I had to go, and I picked up my dice and put them in my pocket. Then X jumped up and said, "What did you pick up those dice for?" I said, "Because I'm finished shooting, and I'm going to split." He said, "You can't quit now; you have to give me a chance to win back some of my money." I couldn't understand him coming down on me with that because I hadn't won that much money. I said, "Hey, man, I'm tired of shooting, and I've got to be somewhere now."

'Then he got right up in my face and said, "You're not quitting yet, motherfucker." I thought to myself, "There's no use trying to talk to him; reasoning with him is out of the question," so I said "The hell if I'm not; I told you that I'm tired of playing." He stared at me with his eyes popping out of his head like he was crazy and said, "You dirty, no-good fucking ass punk." I figured then that I was in a hell of a situation. I knew that the drunken fool wasn't in his right state of mind, and I got scared because I knew he carried a gun and didn't care what he did. I heard that he had killed a dude some time back.

'I said, "Man, will you get the fuck out of my face?" But that sent him into a rage. He started swinging his arms side to side and calling me a motherfucking punk, and he spit in my face. I called him a dirty motherfucker, and he shoved me. I figured then that he wasn't going to be wasting much more time on me, and when he went into his coat I thought that he was reaching for his piece. I knew then that I had to act quick, so I pulled out my pistol and shot the crazy damn fool before he could shoot me. I knew that he'd shoot me without any hesitation. I was just damn lucky that I had bought a gun after being mugged about a week before.'

Restraining judgment

The second event which may occur is a 'restraining judgment.' This occurs when the actor breaks out of a fixed line of indication and decides that he should not carry out his violent plan of action into overt conduct. He *redefines* the situation and on the basis of his new definition of it *now* judges that he should not act violently. Thus, in forming a restraining judgment, the actor completely drops or shelves the violent plan of action which he had built up and his violent interpretation of the situation subsides. The study of these near situations suggests several types of reasons why actors form restraining judgments.[2]

First, an actor may form a restraining judgment in the situation because he fears that he will be unsuccessful. By taking the role of the person whom he had planned to assault, the actor implicitly or explicitly indicates to himself that the other person will retaliate if the actor assaults him. Then by taking the role of a generalized other, the actor implicitly or explicitly indicates to himself that he should not carry out his violent plan of action because he would be unsuccessful in a physical encounter with the other person. Case 34 below is an example of an actor who formed a malefic interpretation and then restrained it for this reason.

Case 34: Near situation

'I was in jail. I saw a newspaper laying open on a table so I sat down and started reading it. Then this dude came up out of nowhere and said, "Don't be fucking with anything on my end of that table." I said, "I don't see any name on this table or that paper." He said, "Everything on this end of the table is mine, and I don't fuck around with niggers or white folks." I thought to myself, "What a sick, stupid motherfucker." As I got up and walked away from the table, I said to this other dude, "What the fuck is wrong with that crazy s.o.b.?'' When he heard me say that, he charged up to me and said, "Motherfucker, you don't have to ask anybody about me." I really didn't want any fight with the dude because he looked pretty bad; he had big old arms and shoulders, and some of his teeth were missing. So I only said, "Man, you must be crazy; what is wrong with your ass?" Then he fired on me. He hit me hard and downed me. Then I saw that he had opened up my fucking nose. I really got hot. I just thought I wanted to kill that dirty s.o.b. I jumped up to my feet and pulled out a fingernail file that I had on me. But then I thought, "This file won't stop him, and he's too fucking big to fight without something more than this. I better back off." After I backed up a few feet, I said, "Motherfucker, don't you ever turn your back near me; you've busted my fucking nose, and I'm going to get you for it." He looked at me and said "Come on, do it right now." I just said, "I'll catch you later" and walked off fast, real fast.'

Second, an actor may form a restraining judgment in the situation because the other person has suddenly changed his line of action. By taking the role of the person whom he had planned to assault, the actor implicitly or explicitly indicates to himself that his or her physically threatening, malicious, or frustrating gestures have been altered or halted. Next, by taking the role of a generalized other, the actor implicitly or explicitly indicates to himself that he no longer needs to carry out his violent plan of action. Case 55 below illustrates an actor who formed a frustrative interpretation and then restrained it for this reason.

Case 55: Near situation

'I needed to score, but my money wasn't right, so I started thinking about where I could get the coin. I decided that I was going to have to go out and rob some fucking place. Then I started thinking about different places to hit. My mind first turned to this Dairy Queen, but I figured that it wouldn't be worth the trouble since there wouldn't be much money there anyway. Then I started thinking about this small supermarket, but I dropped that idea for the same reason. Finally a cleaner's flashed in my mind. I figured that it would be the best hit since there would be enough money and only old ladies worked there. I put on my sunglasses, grabbed my .45, took off the safety clip, and headed for the cleaner's. I walked in the place, pulled out my pistol, and pointed it at the old lady behind the counter. I said, "This is a hold-up; I don't want to shoot you, so give me all the money out of that cash register fast." She walked over to the cash register, but then just stopped and said "I'm not going to give you this money" and stepped on a button on the floor.

'I told myself I was going to get that money. I leaned over the counter and put the barrel of my pistol in her face and said, "Lady, now I'm going to kill you." But just as I was going to pull the trigger, she opened the cash register drawer and said, "You can get the money yourself." I then told her to get away from the cash register, and she did. After I grabbed all the paper money, she smiled and said, "I guess I don't know much about you youngsters these days." I looked at her for a moment and thought that she was just a nice old batty grandmother. Then I split fast.'

Third, an actor may form a restraining judgment because he fears that he will seriously damage the social relationship such as friendship or marriage that exists between him and the other person. By taking the role of the person whom he had planned to assault, the actor implicitly or explicitly indicates to himself that this person might end or drastically change his relationship with the actor if he assaults him. Next, by taking the role of a generalized other, he implicitly or explicitly indicates to himself that he should not carry out his violent plan of action because he does not want to jeopardize his social relationship with this person. Case 58 illustrates how an actor who formed a frustrative-malefic interpretation restrained it for this reason.

Case 58: Near situation

'I was at home looking for the t.v. guide when I found a note written by my wife. It said that she owed somebody $6 for babysitting for her twelve hours. I thought to myself "Where in the living hell could she have been gone for twelve hours?" My mind then turned to her stepping out with someone behind my back, so I called her. When she came in the room, I said, "What in the hell is this note about?" She grabbed the note out of my hand and said, "Oh, it's nothing." I said, "What in the hell do you mean that it's nothing? Where in the hell were you for twelve hours?"

'Then she started giving me some story about going shopping and to the hairdresser's. I said, "Bullshit, that crap doesn't take any twelve hours to do." She said, "Well, maybe the twelve hours that I

33

wrote on the note is a mistake." I said, "Don't hand me that bullshit; you're fucking around with someone." She said, "No, no, I'm not." Then I yelled, "You no-good tramp, dirty whore, you better tell me where in the hell you have been." She said, "You are acting like nothing but a bum; I'm not going to tell you anything." I thought to myself, "I'm going to beat the damn truth out of that no-good, rotten bitch." I started thinking about tying her up and beating her until she talked, but then I thought that if I went that far, she might leave me, so I dropped it. I was scared that if I did do it, then I would end up losing her.'

Fourth, an actor may form a restraining judgment out of deference to another person. By taking the role of a person who is important to him, the actor implicitly or explicitly indicates to himself that this person does not desire him to act violently. Next, by taking the role of a generalized other, the actor implicitly or explicitly indicates to himself that he should not carry out his violent plan of action because he wants to respect this person's wishes. Case 32 below is an example of an actor who formed a malefic interpretation and then restrained it for this reason.

Case 32: Near situation

'I was at a bar where I used to spend a lot of time when the bartender told me that X had come in earlier looking for me. I didn't think too much about it at the time, but a little while later she came back. As soon as she saw me, she charged up to me and said, "Bitch, I've been looking for you; what in the hell did you think you were doing running out on me the other night?" I looked at her and thought to myself, "This bulldagging bitch must think she owns me. I don't have to own up to her or anybody else." Then she said, "Well, bitch, what have you got to say for yourself?" I had had enough of her phony ass then, and I said, "Bitch, you better get out of my face; you don't control what I do; I do what I please." She said, "Bitch, you better watch how you talk to me, 'cause I'll get into your ass." My mind turned to cutting her then and doing it fast. I grabbed my razor and said, "Bitch, I'm going to cut you up so bad that they won't be able to sew your ass up." But before I could get to her with it, Y jumped in between us and said, "Be cool; don't be doing anything like that." I really wanted to hurt that bitch, but out of due respect to Y, I dropped it. If he hadn't asked me to leave her alone, I would have cut her ass up so bad it wouldn't have been funny.'

And fifth, an actor may form a restraining judgment because he fears possible legal sanction. By taking the role of other persons, he indicates to himself that they will witness his assault on the intended victim. Next, by taking the role of a generalized other, he implicitly or explicitly indicates to himself that he should not carry out his violent plan of action since he does not want to be arrested or incarcerated. Case 54 illustrates an actor who formed a frustrative interpretation and then restrained it for this reason.

Case 54: Near situation

'I was doing some Christmas shopping at a shopping center in my neighborhood. I was going through the stores looking for things to get for my family when I started picking up on the women shopping near me. Then I just stopped in the middle of the shopping plaza and looked at the women who walked by. While I was standing there checking them out good, my dick got on a bad hard. I was tripping on butt fucking some of the broads who walked by with real nice plump asses and slim waists when the idea came to me to rip one of them off. I decided to do it, so I went and stole a carving knife from a grocery store and then walked out to the corner of the parking lot of the shopping center. I wanted to find a broad with a nice full ass walking alone to her car. I figured that I'd jump into her car with her and then make her drive out to a deserted area nearby that I knew about. I was watching people going to their cars when I spotted this broad with a nice face and big hips and a fat round ass walking by herself. She looked like an easy rip-off, so I started following her and snuck up right behind her. When she stuck her keys in her car door, I grabbed her by the arm, flashed my knife in her face and said, "Get into your car and don't make any noise." She just stood there like she was in a complete daze. So I let go of her arm and grabbed her car keys and opened the car door myself. I told her to get in because we were going for a ride, but she just started screaming her ass off. First I decided to force her into the car, and I grabbed onto her again, but she kept on screaming and started getting away from me. I figured that other people were probably seeing by now what was happening, so I thought I had

35

better get the hell out of there fast before I got busted. Then I booked it, and she ran off toward the stores screaming.'

Overriding judgment

The final event which may occur is an 'overriding judgment.' This occurs when the actor breaks out of a fixed line of indication and either momentarily considers restraining his violent plan of action or actually forms a restraining judgment but then he redefines the situation and rejudges it as definitely calling for violent action. After forming a violent interpretation of the situation, the actor restrains his violent plan of action; but then he *again* redefines the situation and judges that he should now go ahead and carry out the plan of action into overt conduct. The study of *completed* violent situations suggests that the primary reason why actors form over-riding judgments is because they judge the victim's conduct to be *intolerable*. By taking the role of the victim, the actor implicitly or explicitly indicates to himself that the victim is continuing his frus-trating or malicious line of action. Then by taking the role of a generalized other, the actor implicitly or explicitly indicates to himself that he should go ahead and carry out his violent plan of action because the victim's gestures have become intolerable. Case 32 below illustrates how an actor overruled a restraining judgment for this reason after she had formed a malefic interpretation.[3]

Case 32 (aggravated assault)

'We were partying one night in my rooms at the hotel where I lived and worked. Everybody there was a regular, except for this one dude who I had rented a room down the hall. He just kind of drifted in, and X said that he knew the dude, so it was cool. We were all drinking wine, taking pills, and having a mellow time when I over-heard this dude asking X who I was and saying that I was a bitch. I said, "Hey, who's the bitch you are talking about?" and he said "You're the bitch." I thought to myself, "What does this dude think he's doing coming to my party uninvited and then calling me a fucking bitch?" I said, "Don't you come to my party and call me a bitch." He said, "You are a bitch; I was high and you shortchanged me out of fucking $20 when I paid you for my room today." I said, "Man, you are crazy." He said, "Don't try to slick me, bitch; I'm hip; I'm an ex-con; I know what's happening and X knows I'm good people, so don't try to run that game on mc."

'My friends were having a good time, I felt good, and I didn't want to spoil the mood for any problems behind $20, so I thought that I'd just pacify the chump and give him a lousy $20 and end it. I said, "Look, man, I didn't shortchange you out of any money today, but just to show my good heart, I'll give you $20; how about that?" He said, "Well, since you needed it so fucking bad that you had to try to run a game like that past me, then you can keep it, bitch." Then I thought that motherfucker was just messing with me. He was trying to make me out as a petty hustler and call me a bitch right in front of my friends. I said to myself, "Please, motherfucker, don't mess with me any more." I finally said, "Mister, I'm warning you, don't you fuck with me any more or I'll show you what a fucking bitch is." He just looked at me, laughed and said, "I haven't seen the bitch yet who could kick my ass."

'Then I told myself, "This man has got to go one way or another; I've just had enough of this motherfucker messing with me; I'm going to cut his dirty motherfucking throat." I went into my bedroom, got a $20 bill and my razor. I said to myself, "The motherfucker wouldn't stop fucking with me and now he's hung himself," and I walked out of the bedroom. I went up to him with a big smile on my face. I held the $20 bill in my hand out in front of me and hid the razor in my other hand. Then I sat on his lap and said, "O.K., you're a fast dude; here's your $20 back." He said, "I'm glad that you are finally admitting it." I looked at him with a smile and said, "Let me seal it with a kiss." I said to myself, "Motherfucker, now I'll show you what a fucking bitch is," and then I bent over like I was going to kiss him and started slicing up his throat.'

Case 24 below is another example of an actor who overruled a restraining judgment for this same reason after he had formed a frustrative-malefic interpretation.

Case 24 (aggravated assault)

'My brother and I met this dude at a bar where we were drinking and cutting it up. The dude invited us over to his place to drink some beer after the bar closed. We wanted to crash there for the night. We got a couple of six packs and took a cab over to his pad. Then after we finished drinking all of the beer, the dude dropped the

37

bombshell and said, "Look, you guys are going to have to leave now," I said, "Hell, why didn't you tell us that before we came over here?" He said, "Well, I'm telling you that now." I thought to myself, "We bought the beer, paid for the cab, and haven't gotten out of line; this dude is just using us," so I said, "I'm not going anywhere; there are no buses or cabs running now. I'm not going out on that street hitchhiking this time of night." I was ready to fuck his loud, smart ass up, but my brother said, "Come on, X, let's go." I decided that he was right and I would go on and listen to him and split rather than start a hassle. But then the dude pushed me and said, "You heard what I said, now go on and get the fuck out of here." I said, "Look, don't you push me", but then he pushed me again. I thought, "This smart ass nickel and dime drunk thinks he can just shit all over us" and I told him, "I'm leaving so don't you push me again or I'll fuck you up." Then my brother said, "Come on, let's just go, fuck this dude." The dude said, "That's right, get your fucking ass out of here now", and pushed me once more. I said to myself, "Fuck it, that's it, I'm going to fuck him up." I hit him with a right hook, went beserk, and grabbed a lamp and busted him over the head and downed him. I yelled, "You punk motherfucker, I'll kick your eyes out of your head" and stomped him in the face . . .'

To sum up, in the *completed* violent situations studied here, the actors always either entered into a fixed line of indication or else formed an overriding judgment; whereas in the *near* violent situations that were studied, the actors always formed a restraining judgment. Thus, once actors have formed violent plans of action, whether or not they carry them out depends upon what happens during the process of interpretation, that is, it depends upon whether they stay in a fixed line of indication or form a restraining or overriding judgment.

5 Self as object: self images

Data were gathered on the self images that the fifty-eight offenders held *at the time of their violent offense*. This was done by having them construct objects of themselves for this period of their lives. More fully, the offenders were asked: (1) how they thought of themselves during that time, (2) how they thought others, that is, intimates such as best friends, spouses, etc. thought of them during that time, and (3) if how these others saw them was accurate and why or why not. Study of these data suggests that the self images of actors who have committed violent criminal acts, i.e., substantial violent acts, fall into three types: *violent, incipient violent,* and *non-violent.*[1]

Violent

Violent self images are those in which the actors are seen by others and judge themselves as having a *violent disposition*, i.e., a willingness or readiness to actually respond with physical violence toward other persons, as well as having violence related personal attributes (such as being mean, ill-tempered, hot-headed, explosive, forceful, etc.) as a *salient* characteristic. Case 35 below illustrates a man in his early twenties who was convicted of aggravated assault and who held a violent self image at the time of his offense.

Case 35 (aggravated assault)

'I was a low-rider. I loved to get loaded and drive fast or just kick back and listen to hard rock, drink wine, smoke dope, and wrench my high-powered motor. I liked anything mechanical that went fast. I was free-wheeling; one day I'd be in Frisco, the next in San Diego, putting, wired up, all night long. I did plenty of good fucking too. My old lady worked, so I could just lay back and watch the river go by. Every now and then, though, I'd have to supplement what she brought home with some heavy hustling of my own, like armed robberies and other things. My old lady and ace partner both thought I was a good heavy hustling motherfucker.

'When I got bored with all that then, I might go out scrapping. I was a quiet dude, but enjoyed touching up a dude that was loud. If I heard a dude talking loud about a lot of shit, it upset me inside. Once that happened, I wanted to get it on, check out the dude's oil and find out if he was a quart low. I was not often ever scared of anybody or anything. I'd seen life come and go.

'My number one old lady thought more or less the same about me. She thought if I could just cage my temper that I wouldn't be a half bad guy. She knew when I was hot, I was a mad animal, and even when I was cool, I still acted like a barbarian. I was just the loosest motherfucker that she ever met; she thought I just didn't give a fuck about a thing. I spent money too freely, used too many drugs, and nutted up too much. People used to wonder how come a fine foxy woman like her put up with a dude like me, but she did. I was her main squeeze and she never went south on me.

'My acetramp partner thought of me as a pretty jam-up dude. He knew that I'd always back his play and that there would never be any slack on my part. He thought that I was just a low-rider at heart who just liked to get loaded, ride fast and fight. He thought that I was down with it when it came to hopping up motors, and that I didn't fuck with any dogs. He also knew the three things that I gave a fuck about and didn't let anybody mess with—my old lady, my kid, and my motorcycle.

'Nothing else really mattered to me. The philosophy that I followed was that you do whatever you want to do, when and how you want to do it and fuck everything and everybody else. This meant to me that you had the most balls, you did the most outrageous things; in other words, that you were one of the most terrible motherfuckers who ever walked the streets. I was caught up in trying to live up to this twenty-four hours a day. That was me.'

Participant-observation case 1 below illustrates a man in his late forties who held a violent self image. He has committed many substantial violent acts in which the police became involved and some of which I observed. This case is particularly important because it illustrates the violent self image of an actor who had not undergone any prison socialization.

Participant-Observation Case 1

'I'm X the [nationality]. I'm a man, not a boy, and I don't need any titty bottle to suck on. I want to be treated like a man too. I don't go humming around people's houses and asking them, "What you got to eat?" I don't eat over at other people's houses period. People know that I got groceries in my icebox. I don't have my old lady working either. I buy all the groceries and pay the bills in my house, so what I say goes. It better damn sight go. I'm the king of my house, and if somebody doesn't like it, then they can just get the fuck out. There are no locks on my doors. I don't care how other people run their houses. If someone is living under my roof and eating my food, then they better do what I say whether they like it or not. And they all know it too.

'I'm a hardworking s.o.b., and I deserve some respect for it. I work a regular job, but I make my livelihood by working on the side too. I'm a natural hustler. I know how to talk to people. I was born with the gift of gab. I can sell anybody. I can go out there anytime and make myself some extra money. I don't need any college degrees or union cards to do it either. I don't need to wait for payday every week to get my money. I can make it on any day of the week. I don't give a damn how many union cards or degrees a person has; I can outmake them three to one. Shit, I can go out there and make in one day what those poor bastards slave to make all week; and if I have a good day, I can make more money than they'll make in a month. I don't have to ask people to lend me a couple of bucks till payday. I don't have to go around saying that I have this or that degree or union card; I just flash the roll in my wallet. Talk is cheap. Money is what talks in this world, and my mind is always on how to make a buck.

'I just don't have time for hobbies and mess like most people do. I got too many mouths to feed. Everybody in my house is depending on me and on what I bring home, so I don't waste my time collecting things, talking about politics, and reading the paper or books trying to impress people with how much I know. That horseshit won't buy you anything. While those people are sitting on their fat asses talking about this or that or messing around with their hobbies, I'm out there making a buck. I'm no fool or dummy.

'Of course, this doesn't mean that I don't ever like to have fun. I'll lay a bet or two on the world series, superbowl and things like that. I also enjoy taking a sociable drink every day, but I'm not a drunk. I don't stay out of work drunk, and you won't find me staggering around my house or falling out in the damn street. I'm no wino, and I have never been one. I'm not what you would call a sick alcoholic, like some people I know.

'I'm a man and I want to be treated like a man. Hell, I'm real easy to get along with just as long as people don't take me too light. I just don't play. When I tell somebody something, I mean it. I don't want to hear a whole lot of horseshit about who did what. I don't care who a person is or who they think they are either; they better not play around with me. I'll show them who in the hell they're playing with. They'll find out fast that they aren't fucking with any boy when they fuck with me. I'll put my foot in their ass quick. Once I get started on them, I'll fix their ass up right. I've ruined more than one good man in my time, and, Jack, I'll do it again too. That's the way I am, and that's the way I'll be until the day that I die. Everybody knows that's the way I am.'

Incipient violent

Incipient violent self images are those in which the actors are seen by others and judge themselves as having an *incipient violent disposition*, i.e., a willingness or readiness to make serious threats of violence, such as violent ultimatums and menacing physical gestures, to other persons, as well as having violence related personal attributes, as a *salient* characteristic. The difference between violent and incipient violent self images is that in the former the actor is seen by others and judges himself as definitely and genuinely being violent, whereas in the latter, this is still problematic, that is, *perhaps* 'more show than go.' An example should make clearer the character of an incipient violent self image. Case 28 below illustrates a woman in her early forties who was convicted of criminal homicide and who held an incipient violent self image at the time of her offense.

Case 28 (criminal homicide)

'I didn't care about anything. I let myself go completely. My appearance was bad. I didn't fix my hair, put on make-up, or care about my clothes. I wasn't attractive to men any more. I used ugly language and drank all the time. I couldn't do my job at home as a mother or at the place where I worked.

'My boss knew my work wasn't as good as it used to be; he thought I was slipping. My work was sliding downhill bad. My husband saw me as an ugly old hag. He said I was just a piece of a woman because I had had a hysterectomy, and he had no more sexual desire for me. He and my oldest daughter both thought I was just a bitchy old woman and an alcoholic who made molehills into mountains. All of the kids felt that I was just an old crab who hollered all the time. I guess I was despicable.

'I was a bitter and bad-tempered person. I couldn't accomplish anything, and nothing that I tried seemed ever to work out. I was full of hate. I wasn't desired by anybody, and my husband didn't have any attraction for me. I felt rejected and like a stupid fool for letting my husband mistreat me. I was getting fed up and easily angered by things. I made a lot of awful threats to people, but they thought it was mostly just big talk. Everybody thought that I would do little real action besides get drunk, scream and cuss, and throw things at people until I passed out.'

Non-violent

Non-violent self images are those in which the actors are not seen by others and do not judge themselves as having a violent or incipient violent disposition as one of their *salient* characteristics. In these self images, non-violence related personal attributes such as good-humored, shy, lazy, personable, boring, obnoxious, etc., make up the salient characteristics of the actor. Case 48 illustrates a woman in her early twenties who was convicted of aggravated assault and who held a non-violent self image at the time of her offense.

Case 48 (aggravated assault)

'I was a young and serious-minded married woman and a perfect lady. People thought I had class. I wore fine dresses and minks, gold rings and was a singer in my man's band. My girlfriend who sang with me saw me as a beautiful person. She thought my personality was nice and that I was a pretty, cat-eyed broad who could really catch dudes' eyes, but she knew I didn't play that game. The dudes in the band saw me as a beautiful person too. They thought that I was sexy and they considered me a good singer. They knew that I could socialize with people real good and felt that I was real nice to work with. They thought that I was a classy broad.

'My husband thought that I was a young and pretty woman and real good to get down with since he said that I had a pussy as tight as a little baby. In fact, he more or less thought of me as innocent because I hadn't learned all the ropes yet, but he still thought that I had a lot of sense for my age. He considered me a pretty good wife and he knew that I had enough class for him to take me anywhere. I was intelligent and a good conversationalist and hostess. He knew that I didn't bite my tongue about anything either. I spoke my mind. I just wanted to have a family, be a mother, and live a nice life. I felt like a lady and wanted to be treated like a lady, but my husband was getting crazy and then embarrassing me in front of everybody behind his jealousy.'

6 Self as object and process: the linkage between self images and interpretations

According to the theoretical perspective used here, the kind of self image one holds should be interlinked with the types of interpretations that he forms of situations which confront him. In the fifty-eight cases at hand, an invariant linkage was found between the types of self images that these actors held at the time of their offense and the types of interpretations that they formed of the situations in which they committed the violent criminal act. More fully, the actors who held non-violent self images only committed their violent criminal acts in situations in which they formed physically defensive interpretations. Those holding incipient violent self images only committed their violent criminal acts in situations in which they formed physically defensive interpretations or frustrative-malefic ones. Finally, those holding violent self images committed violent criminal acts in situations in which they formed malefic, frustrative, frustrative-malefic, as well as physically defensive interpretations.

This interlinkage between non-violent, incipient violent, and violent self images and the various types of interpretations can be illustrated by examples of the actors' self images in conjunction with their interpretations of situations in which they committed violent criminal acts. Case 5 represents a man in his early twenties with a non-violent self image and the physically defensive interpretation that he formed of the situation in which he committed a criminal homicide.

Case 5: Self image (aggravated assault)

'My family thought I was a hard worker who provided exceptionally well. They knew that I was highly motivated, a person who wanted to learn. I believed you could get anything you wanted if you knew something and knew it well. I knew you had to have a bill of goods to sell. People saw me as a guy who knew a trade and knew it well. I could sell myself anytime. I always had something to offer. I would sell an image of doing a great job when I was only working up to one-half of my potential. It was a short cut way to get the most. I had my own style.

'I loved self accomplishment. I was a perfectionist. I wanted to make it before I was forty, make it while I was young; that was what I tried to do. I thought I had done it. I had pride in myself.

'People saw me as Mr—. I was a neat dresser. I loved money and what it would buy to an extreme people didn't realize. I liked luxury, $200 suits, diamonds, etc. There was nothing else. That was where it was at. I was hip to what was happening. Nobody could get an angle on me.'

Interpretation 'X and I were getting a divorce and my lawyer advised me to move out of the house. I went home to get some of my things out of the basement.

'I heard X coming down the steps while I was packing my stuff to leave and first glanced at X when X was at the middle of the steps. I figured X was coming down to talk. But when X didn't say a word to me, I stopped packing and turned toward X. I saw that X had a boning knife. I thought that X was trying to steal me, stab me on the sly, while my back was turned. I jumped over a box into the corner and X started coming fast, fast, fast. I knew X was going to try to kill me. I took the gun from the bag that I had just packed and fired.'

Case 57 below represents a man in his mid-thirties with an incipient violent self image and the frustrative-malefic interpretation that he formed of the situation in which he committed a criminal homicide.

Case 57: Self image (criminal homicide)

'I was a good provider for my family and a hard worker. My boss considered me a much better than average employee. He thought that I was a reliable, loyal, and honest worker. Many customers even called and said how nice and polite a driver that I was. I got along good with everybody. My boss knew that I was a very reserved individual and never said anything out of the way to people.

'My wife thought that I was boring and a narrow man because my interests and time were completely monopolized by sports and t.v. It disgusted her that all I wanted to do was come home, take my shirt off, sip on a beer, eat, and watch t.v. and then go to different sports events on the weekends with my kids. The kids always had fun doing it. The sports world was all that I liked, and I had nothing to say that didn't have something to do with it. I didn't care for any intellectual type things, and my wife knew it. She also called me anti-social, but I always got along good with all the people that I came into contact with. I just didn't want any intimate after-hours relationships with any of them. I didn't care about things like friends coming over.

'My wife thought that I was physically unattractive too. She said I was a slob because I wouldn't keep myself neat and clean and dressed up. When I came home from work, I was tired and wanted to relax. I didn't feel like shaving and showering and changing right away like she wanted. She thought that I was a poor husband period.

'She said that I was too rigid and bossy. She felt that I forced her to accept all my decisions with threats about what I would do if she didn't. I know I sure frightened her when I got mad because I did let her know that she better damn well accept my decisions and not complain about it too much. I was a hardworking man, a good provider, and generous to my family, so there shouldn't have been any complaints from her about who gave the orders, what I did, and the rest. But I still had to let her know from time to time that she better not take her crap too far.'

Interpretation 'I was out of town, and I called my wife one night to check on what was going on at home. She told me that she had seen an attorney and was filing papers to divorce me. I asked her to hold off until I got back home and could sit down and talk it over with her, but she said, "No, this time I really mean it." After she told me that, I blew up and said, "You better not do that to me; if you do, you'll be sorry for it." She said, "I had a restraining order placed on you, so if you come around here bothering me, the police will get you." I said, "If I really want to get you, the police can't save you." I thought that telling her that would scare her, but it didn't. She just

47

acted calm and confident like she had everything all planned out. That got me madder. I knew then that it was no use raising any more hell over the 'phone since it wasn't intimidating her. I figured that I had to get home and confront her face to face. I just felt plain mad. I hung up the 'phone and headed straight for home. I wanted to see if she would talk as brave about a divorce to me when I got home as she did over the 'phone.

'When I did get home three hours later, she was in bed asleep. I woke her up and told her to get up, that I wanted to talk. I told her if she stopped with the divorce, and that I would promise to act better and . . . but she wouldn't buy any of it. I got angrier and angrier. Then she came out and said, "Look, please do me this favor and give me a divorce." At that moment I felt cold hatred for her inside me. I told myself that I better leave before I exploded on her, but then I decided the hell with it, and I looked at her straight in the face and said, "Well, X, you better start thinking about those poor kids of ours." She said, "I don't care about them; I just want a divorce."

'My hate for her exploded then, and I said, "You dirty, no-good bitch", and started pounding her in the face with my fist. She put her arms up and covered her face, so I ran and got my rifle and pointed it at her. I said, "Bitch, you better change your mind fast or I'm going to kill you." She looked up and said in a smart-ass way, "Go ahead then, shoot me." I got so mad and felt so much hate for her, that I just started shooting her again and again . . .'

Case 29 below illustrates a woman in her late twenties with a violent self image and the malefic interpretation that she formed of the situation in which she committed an aggravated assault.[1]

Case 29: Self image (aggravated assault)

'I would have been best described as a "femme fatale." Many men were sexually attracted to me, and I was sexually attracted to many different men. The men that I knew saw me as a sweet, cute, and sexy woman who loved to party, and they knew that I was loose too. But I was unsure about myself. I was an emotionally unstable person. I would usually act nice and be sweet, but I could get really hateful too. Once I did get real mad, I blew it, and I would do anything to somebody. Some people realized that when I went crazy, I was dangerous.

'My old man thought I had a delicious body and was a good baller, but he called me a chump and a whore a lot of times. He knew I liked to run around, go bar hopping, get myself loaded or drunk and ball. My girlfriends knew that I liked to sneak around too. I did love sex, all kinds, and a whole lot of it. I was a nymph, so what?

'I was also a top waitress. I kept a clean house, and I cooked good and tried to be a good mother to my kids too, although I felt guilty sometimes for not spending more time with them.'

Interpretation 'My boyfriend and I were bickering when he announced to me that he had decided to go back to his wife and was going to pack his bags and leave. He said that now that he had a job making good money, she would take him back, and that he thought that they could make it together. I said, "Then you better give me some money for living here the last two months free and pay me back all the money that I've loaned you too." He said, "I don't owe you a damn penny for living here, and I don't have to pay you back any of that money you gave me." I said, "You dirty s.o.b., you don't give a damn about me; you've just been using me all along, haven't you?" He didn't give me an answer; he just acted cool and ignored me. I said to myself, "He can't get away with pulling this after all the things that he has already done to me; he broke up my relationship with X; he lived here free; he took my money, ruined my car . . . He has just done too much to me to get away with it." I said, "Don't think that you are going to get away with this that easy," and he just got up and said he was packing his things. Then I started thinking about what I could do to get him. Poison him? No, he's not going to want to be eating anything now; I guess I have to shoot him. Then I thought I better not because I'd get into a lot of trouble for it, but finally I told myself, "Enough is enough; I'm going to do it. I don't care if I do get in trouble." While I was still worked up and had the nerve, I went and got the pistol that my old boyfriend had left in the house. Then I walked up to him and said, "You dirty rotten s.o.b." He said, "Please don't shoot me." I said to myself, "You yellow punk, you never stopped beating me when I asked you," and I shot him.'

And finally, case 9 below illustrates a man in his late twenties with a violent self image and the frustrative interpretation that he formed of the situation in which he committed a forcible rape.

49

Case 9: Self image (forcible rape)

'Most people thought I was a good guy who always took care of his family and was a good provider and worker. I was loved by most everybody – my wife, kids, in-laws, and the guys I went around with. My father-in-law said that I was the best son-in-law that he had. They all liked me because I joked and laughed a lot.

'They knew that I was a happy-go-lucky guy who minded my own business, but they knew that I was a man and when I got to drinking, look out. You couldn't tell me anything. I did what I wanted no matter what it took. I was a crazy lunatic then and got real mean. My wife would get scared of me when I was drinking too because I would hit her one time too many. Everybody said that alcohol made me become a lunatic. I know that it got me twenty years.

'I was a real man who liked to gamble around, do some drinking, and search for pussy. I was a searcher, married or single. What women got, their curves and shapes, I liked and needed. I would take it any way that I could. I didn't like anybody interfering with my getting pussy. I'd beat them good if they did. I was a pussy-raper. I believed in taking pussy by my might or whatever else it took to get it.

'If I had twenty girls, I'd fuck every one of them. I got tired of sex with one woman. I knew a man could go out, search and take pussy and not lose his respect. I believed a man has the right to a woman's beauty. When I saw it, I wanted it. I liked to be the first man to top a new pussy to boot. Pussy was always on my mind. The guys I went around with knew it and they looked for it too. I was a searcher, a real man, and a good fucking guy.'

Interpretation   'I hadn't had any pussy for some time so I felt horny as shit. Then I started thinking about this girl I met at a party a couple of weeks ago. She was built thin but enough meat was on her to throw it up to me good. She never acted interested in me, but I had heard that her and the older woman in her building were giving up boatloads of pussy. I was drunk and my mind was on pussy so I headed for their place. (I found out from a friend where they lived.) When I got there, I noticed the older woman in her room with the door wide open so I went in and said hi. She asked me what I wanted. I said I wanted sex and decided to try to talk her into fucking first. But she said, "I'm not going to do anything like that with you," so I knew then I was just going to take it. I said, "Yes,

50

you are" and beat on her but she still wouldn't give open so I got the pipe . . .'

In short, actors with non-violent self images commit violent criminal acts (i.e., substantial violent acts) only on the basis of physically defensive interpretations; those with incipient violent self images do so only on the basis of physically defensive or frustrative-malefic ones; whereas actors with violent self images do so on the basis of any of the four types of interpretations here posited.[2] Thus, actors with violent and incipient violent self images interpret a wider range of situations as calling for violence than do those with non-violent ones.

7 Careers of violent actors

According to the theoretical perspective used here, the careers of violent actors evolve around their self images and violent histories. Data were gathered on these topics for thirty-five of the violent offenders. This was done by asking them two sets of questions. The first set of questions dealt with the offenders' self images. They were asked how they saw themselves at the time of their offense, how they thought others saw them during that time period, if how these others saw them was accurate and why or why not, and finally, how long, or between what approximate ages, they saw themselves and thought others saw them in this way. The second set of questions dealt with the offenders' past violent acts. They were asked to describe all the past violent acts which they had perpetrated during the period of their lives that they held the self image just described. They were also asked to particularly note the degree of injury they inflicted upon the other person, approximately how old they were when they committed the act, and whether or not the police actually contacted them with regard to it.

The offenders were then asked the same sets of questions for an *earlier* time of their lives *ending* with the period in which they held the self image and committed the violent acts just described. These two sets of questions were repeated for still earlier time periods of the offenders' lives until they could no longer provide answers to the questions about their self images. When this point was reached in the questioning, they said such things as 'To tell you the truth, I don't remember much about how I saw myself or how other people, saw me back then, or 'Before that I saw myself as just another kid, and I guess everybody else saw me as just a kid too; that's about it.'

The study of these data suggests several things. First, it suggests that the self images these actors held over their lives fall into the same basic types previously described — violent, incipient violent, and non-violent. Secondly, it suggests that the period of their lives when they held these types of self images fall into three types — *substantial violent, unsubstantial violent*, and *negligible violent*.

Substantial violent periods are marked by actors having perpetrated at least one, but often more, substantial violent acts which were not victim precipitated, or committed as a result of forming a physically defensive interpretation. Substantial violent acts have either of two qualities: (1) the victim is substantially physically injured, i.e., deliberately injured either fatally or to a degree that usually calls for a physician's attention, such as results from a shooting, stabbing, clubbing, or relentless beating, or (2) the victim is substantially sexually violated, as in the case of coitus, sodomy, fellatio, or cunnilingus, either under the threat of the infliction of substantial physical injury or the actual infliction of substantial or unsubstantial physical injury.

Unsubstantial violent periods are marked by actors having perpetrated several unsubstantial violent acts, but no substantial violent acts which were not victim precipitated. Unsubstantial violent acts have either of three qualities: (1) the victim is unsubstantially physically injured, i.e., deliberately physically injured to a degree that usually does not call for a physician's attention, such as results from being slapped, backhanded, pushed, mildly punched, choked, or kicked; or (2) the victim is unsubstantially sexually violated, i.e., to a degree short of coitus, sodomy, fellatio, or cunnilingus; or (3) the victim is not actually substantially physically injured but is seriously threatened with substantial injury, as in the case of verbally threatening to physically injure someone while displaying or discharging a dangerous weapon when substantial sexual violation does not take place.[1]

Finally, negligible violent periods are marked by actors having perpetrated no substantial and very few, if any, unsubstantial violent acts which were not victim precipitated.

The third thing that the study of these data suggests is that the type of self images the offenders held over their lives are correlated with the types of violent periods they had. More fully, when the actors held violent self images, they had substantial violent periods. When they held incipient violent self images, they had unsubstantial violent periods. And finally, when they held non-violent self images, they had negligible violent periods. This correlation will be illustrated in the examples which follow shortly.

The final thing that the study of these data suggests is that the careers of violent actors fall into three basic types – *stable*, *escalating*, and *de-escalating*. These career types will now be examined.

Stable

The first type of career which violent actors have, a stable career, is where the type of self images and violent periods that an actor has had over his life stay the same. Within this type of career, actors were found whose self images and violent periods were always violent and substantial violent or always non-violent and negligible violent. It is noteworthy that no one was found whose self images and violent periods were always incipient violent and unsubstantial violent. This suggests that incipient violent self images and unsubstantial violent periods may be more transitory than the other types. Persons who are in unsubstantial violent periods of their lives and hold incipient violent self images apparently begin perpetrating substantial violent acts and develop violent self images or else they stop perpetrating unsubstantial violent acts and develop non-violent self images. It makes sense that these persons either stop making threats and attempts to seriously injure or sexually violate other persons or actually carry out these threats and attempts, since it is likely that other persons will sooner or later challenge them to do so.

Case 56 illustrates the stable violent career of a man who was convicted of criminal homicide.

Case 56, Age 9–14: Violent self image

'I was very mature and perceptive beyond my years and I had a lot of freedom. I went backpacking and camped out by myself regularly. I knew the realities of life too. I always had chores around the house and I did them. I also always did odd jobs after school to earn my own spending money and I worked at odd jobs all summer long. I believed at a young age that a person should work for what he gets. I was super intelligent and a bold kid too. I would often manipulate grown-ups to my advantage without them even knowing it, and I had gotten drunk several times. I was very mischievious but not offensive where grown-ups were concerned. My folks considered me to be a real good kid.

'I had a little temper too, and after my grandfather taught me how to fight, I was the cock of the walk at school. I believed in always standing my ground, but not to push people off theirs. I was proud that there were kids sixteen and seventeen who wouldn't fuck with me. I tried to follow the code of fair play and fighting that my grandfather instilled in me: "It is worse to win a fight if you're wrong than to get your ass whipped if you are right. But if you are right, then no holds are barred. If fists don't work, then don't box. Pick up a rock, baseball bat, anything. A bully doesn't deserve a boxing match anyway, but anything that he gets." I didn't always follow this since sometimes I was the bully, but I always kept in mind that a man should have whatever he asks for. Everybody knew that I would really fight and when I got into a fight I didn't ever play. I would fistfight or do whatever else was needed to win.'

Age 9–14: Substantial violent period

Age 9: Substantial violent act 'I came home from school with my knees all skinned up and my trousers ripped. My grandfather asked me what happened. I told him that a big black kid beat me up at recess. He said that he didn't want any nigger beating up his grandson and then began giving me boxing lessons. I jumped the kid the next day at recess, but he downed me again. When I told my grandfather about it, he whipped me and then told me that I better beat that kid's ass the next day or he was going to whip me even harder. I knew that kid couldn't hurt me as much as my grandfather could, so I tried to whip his ass again. I fired on him at recess and hit him as hard as I could in the face and downed him. While he was down, I kicked him in the head and face good and hard and bloodied his mouth and broke his nose. Then I took his place at school after that as the cock of the walk. I was sent home from school that day. No police.'

Age 11: Substantial violent act 'I started a bad fistfight with this kid a lot older than me. After we exchanged maybe a dozen hard punches, I wanted to quit. I told him that I wanted to throw in the towel, but he wouldn't stop punching me. Finally I broke and ran, but he started running after me. So then I really got mad and stopped and picked up a large stone and busted him in the head.

55

I opened up his forehead bad and he needed ten stitches. No police.'

Age 12: Substantial violent act 'This guy followed me and my friend to my house after school. We were in front of an old shed in my backyard when he picked a fight with my friend. I told the guy to get out of my yard, but he wouldn't leave, so I punched him in the face. He then got mad and picked up a wagon axle and told me to keep out of it. I decided then that I was still going to get him out of my yard so I grabbed a steel pipe out of the shed and swung it at him as hard as I could. It knocked the axle that he was holding out of his hand and then hit his arm and broke it. I didn't get into any trouble behind it.'

Age 13: Substantial violent act 'Two guys and I were playing darts out back of my house. I told them both that they had better not throw any darts at the house since I had gotten into trouble behind doing it, but one of the guys did it anyway. I picked up a two-by-four and told him that he better not do it again. He did and I got mad and hit him as hard as I could in the face with it. I broke his nose and he got stitches in the face. No police.'

Age 14: Substantial violent act 'We had just finished supper, and my stepfather told my brother to wash the dishes, but he refused. My stepfather was drunk, and he started throwing dishes off the table. My mother tried to clear the table before he broke all the dishes, and he smacked her in the face. My brother got up and ran for the back door, but my stepfather cut him off and told him not to leave the kitchen. My mind was on getting out of there as fast as I could before he got on me. I got up from the table, but he pushed me back down in my chair and said, "You better not move from that chair until I tell you or I'll beat your ass good just like I did on your birthday." My mother and brother cleared the dishes left on the table and started washing them. He just stood there glaring at us until the dishes were done. Then he told us all to go into the living room. He bolted the front door shut, and my brother turned on the t.v. My stepfather then turned it off so hard that he broke the knob clean off, and he began yelling at my brother again about the dishes. Finally, I asked my stepfather if I could please go to my room and lay down since I wasn't feeling well. He told me it was O.K., so I went to my room.

'A couple of minutes later he came into my room and said, "You know, you're damn lucky you're sick because you were the one who should have done those dishes." Then there was a crash in the living room, and he ran in there and checked it out. My baby brother had knocked over a lamp, and my stepfather smacked him for it. My baby brother started crying, and my stepfather told my mother, "You better shut that little bastard up." The fear of him that I felt inside then turned to cold hate and anger. The thought came in my mind to kill him. My .22 rifle then flashed in my mind. I got frightened just at the thought of it. I told myself that tonight I was going to kill him.

'My mind turned back to my rifle. My stepfather had taken the bolt out of it and put it in his dresser drawer. I just sat there on my bed and tried to figure out a way that I could get into his room without him catching me. Then my mother said, "X, go get the baby's pacifier off the green dresser in my room." I hesitated. The thought of actually going into their room where my rifle bolt was scared me. My stepfather then yelled, "Didn't you hear your mother, boy? Go get that pacifier." I walked into their room. First I got the rifle bolt out of his drawer. I put it in my pocket and pulled out my shirt to cover it. Then I got the pacifier and went into the living room. When I walked by my stepfather to give my mother the baby's pacifier, I trembled, and he noticed it and thought that it was from fear of walking by him, but it was mostly from the rifle bolt and what I had in my mind to do. My looking scared must have satisfied him good because he told me that I could go back to my room and rest.

'As soon as I did, I put the bolt in my rifle and got some shells out of my sock drawer. As I loaded the rifle, I started thinking about what would happen if I fired and missed him and what would happen if I shot and killed him. I wondered if I'd go to prison. Finally, I decided that I should kill him, so I grabbed my rifle and walked into the hallway and then turned around and walked back into my room. I did this over and over again until finally I got up enough nerve to walk into the living room. My stepfather was sitting on the sofa. I pointed my rifle straight at him and just stood there looking at him. Finally he noticed me, and he jumped up, and I pulled the trigger. I got him in the side, and he fell back down on the sofa. I felt relieved. He looked up at me, and I pulled the trigger again. This time I hit him in the neck, and his whole body started quivering, and I pulled the trigger again and got him in the head. He then completely collapsed down on the floor. I felt tranquil. I knew that he was dead. I had to go to the school for boys behind it.'

Age 14½–19: Violent self image

'Everybody at the school for boys knew that I had a murder beef so they were scared of me. Since it was accepted that I could whip anybody's ass there, I was the duke of the cottages. I ran all the fucking cottages and everybody, including the supervisors, knew it. I got the privileges of the rank and I enjoyed them. I was a little con artist too. I mixed my earlier code about fighting with a new attitude that thieving was all right.

'When I left the boys' school, I was a headstrong, wild, and reckless kid. I was game for anything that would make me a lot of money quick. I drove around all over the place robbing and stealing and I got involved in a lot of hair-brained schemes. People saw me as a John Dillinger type gangster. I had balls and would do things that a person in his right mind just wouldn't do. I was insane. I drank too much and got way out of line and if anybody tried to stop me, I'd jump right on them. I usually packed a pistol and would take a shot at a sucker in a minute. I also was an instinctive marksman, so if anybody did provoke me, I was subject to blowing off their goddam head. Everybody who knew me thought I could seriously hurt or shoot and kill somebody.'

Age 14½–19: Substantial violent period

Age 16½: Substantial violent act 'I hadn't been out on parole from my murder beef too long when I got into a hassle with four dudes at a drive-in. This dude came up to my car and started talking smart to my date. I told the punk to beat it, and he came over to my side of the car and cussed at me through the window and told me to try and make him beat it. Then I saw his partners start heading over to my car. I decided to give them what they needed, and I grabbed a hammer that I kept under the front seat and jumped out. I hit one of them square in the head and downed him. The two others then went for me, and I cracked one over the shoulder and the other one in the head and downed both of them. The other dude with them then ran. The police got me, but all the witnesses said that those other dudes started it for no reason, so they decided to drop the case against me. The three dudes that I hit went to the hospital in an ambulance. I fucked them up bad. I fractured one's collar bone and broke the other two's skulls open.'

Age 17: Unsubstantial violent act 'One night I was half drunk and driving kind of slow down a narrow road when the driver behind me started tailgating and beeping his horn. I looked in my rear-view mirror and saw that it was a carload of guys. I got pissed off and decided to slow down some more. When I turned off onto another road, they started following me, so I pulled over and got out of my pickup with my rifle. When they started pulling over their car, I fired several shots at them, and then they turned around and drove off fast. I didn't hit any of them, but I know that I did hit their car a few times. No police.'

Age 18: Substantial violent act 'I got into a hassle with a dude at a beer joint one night. He was being bounced out of the joint for getting too loud. I started laughing and he got pissed off and downed me. He grabbed a beer bottle off the bar and hit me over the top of the head with it. I didn't need any stitches or anything, but I was hurting bad. I had a huge bump on the top of my head. When I finally got myself together, I went looking for him. Finally I drove around his house and noticed the lights were on. As I snuck up to his house, I saw him through a window and I fired my pistol at him several times. I then dead-headed to a gambling house and spent the rest of the night and next morning there with some tight partners of mine. The police arrested me for his murder, but there were no witnesses and I had a solid alibi so they had to cut me loose.'

Age 19: Unsubstantial violent act 'I lived next to this guy whose dog barked all the time and woke me every morning. I told the man that he better shut his dog up, but he never listened. Then one morning when I had a terrible hangover the dog's barking woke me. I got mad, went out and shot the dog dead. The guy came out screaming at me about the police and shit. I pointed my pistol at him and told him that if he didn't shut up that I was going to blast him too. He ran into his house, and I went back to my apartment, packed my clothes, and took off. I never did get arrested for doing it.'

Age 19: Substantial violent act 'I went over to this broad's pad that I knew. The two broads who shared the apartment with her and

59

their boyfriends were there. Their boyfriends started a hassle with me behind my always coming over there drunk and offering the broads booze and shit. I told them that those broads were old enough to decide for themselves whether or not they wanted a drink or anything else. The big one then got mad and told me to beat it. I was half drunk and in no shape to fight that big s.o.b., so I split. I went to a bar where I hung out and ran down what happened to some friends of mine there. I got all worked up about it and decided to go back over to the broads' pad. Two of my friends came along with me, and I sent one of them up to the door to tell the big dude that I wanted to see him outside. As soon as I saw him coming out, I grabbed the hammer from under my car seat. I got out when he came up to the car and hit him square in the head. He grabbed a hold of me as he fell down on his knees, and I smashed him in the head again. Then I hit him several more times in the body. I put him in critical condition and his brain was damaged. I served ten years behind it.'

Age 20–30: Violent self image

'Although I was born with better mental equipment than I had any right to expect (my I.Q. was measured at 137), I still occasionally did real dumb things that got me in big trouble. I was serving a sentence in prison these last ten years for something dumb that I did. But having to do all that time didn't make me a bitter person. I was more happy-go-lucky than most longtermers in the joint. I learned a good trade, had an uncanny skill at it, and got assigned good jobs because of it. I had a way of picking up on the right information and putting two and two together, so that I always knew what was coming down around the joint. In general, I got along all right and was pretty happy in prison.

'I could relate to most people in the place. I was tolerant of many styles and mixed with a variety of people. I had a lot of friends who didn't have anything positive for each other, but I handled it. I was a social chameleon. I hid or changed my true feelings as the occasion demanded. But most people in general trusted me. They knew I would do a guy a favor if I was in a position to. But I also could be a rotten s.o.b. I did some real rank things, but I also did some redeeming things over these years. I always identified with any underdog and hated bullies. I stepped in on occasion and took

60

unnecessary risks to help out guys in bad situations by standing up for them and putting myself on the line for them.

'I was respected by both institutional staff and inmates for the way that I conducted myself and handled my affairs. I was man enough to tell a guy to go get fucked and I always dealt with people on a one-to-one basis. I expected them to do the same with me too. I didn't need any gang or clique to do my business for me; I was strong enough to handle it myself. If push came to shove, then I'd shove. I loved life, but I wasn't scared of death.

'I was ready to kill or die, but I wasn't a stupid asshole about it. I didn't take any bullshit from anybody, but I didn't go out of my way to give it to people either. If I really got out of line, then I would say I was sorry. I didn't put myself on any serious crosses behind dumb bullshit. I knew when it was best to backpaddle and avoid trouble and when to stand up and meet it all the way. I established a heavy reputation around the joint and it kept me from being picked out or stabbed behind any petty bullshit and let me have pretty much a free run.'

Age 20–30: Substantial violent period

Age between early twenties and thirties, exact age withheld: Substantial violent act 'During the ten year stretch that I did in the pen for the ADW, I only got into one hassle where something actually came down. I killed a dude behind ripping off a little kid who I really dug a lot. One cold dude kept putting pressure on this kid to get down with him. Finally the dude and his partners overpowered the kid and fucked him. When I found out what they did to him, I was pissed off, but I held my cool. A few days later I slid up behind the dude who planned it and shoved a shank all the way through his upper back and left it there. Then I quickly snuck away. Nobody even knew that the dude had been stabbed until over an hour later. Nobody saw me kill him and I never advertised before or after it happened that I was out to get the guy so I got away with it clean.'

Case 37 illustrates the stable non-violent career of a man who was convicted of criminal homicide.

Case 37, Age 14–17: Non-violent self image

'I was dreaming about being a famous singer on stage with a band or

61

being a famous basketball player. I was a wild and mischievous young dude. I liked to drink wine and cut it up with the other dudes, and sometimes I cut school. I also shoplifted some. I was having fun with the ladies, too. I was just young, dumb, and full of come. I was all right with the ladies as far as they were concerned and I was concerned. Not too many of them ever rejected me. They thought I was a lover and sweet talker.

'My steady girl thought that I was a nice-looking, attractive cat with a nice personality. I turned her on. She saw me as a nice, sweet dude. She thought that I had a good voice. The dudes at school knew that I was a better than fair young man with the ladies and they considered me a good basketball player and thought I was a great singer. Everybody thought of me as a friendly cat who acted nice to people.

'Besides my grandmother, all of my family thought that I was a nice, decent young man who respected people older than me. They knew that I didn't cause any trouble at home or at school. My grandmother disliked me when she was sober and hated me when she was drunk because she said that I wasn't my father's son. She mistreated me no matter what I did. I felt sorry for myself because I had to live with her and put up with her crazy shit.'

Age 14–17: Negligible violent period

Age 14: Unsubstantial violent act 'A dude who always picked on everybody at school took my comb. I asked him to give me my comb back and he told me to try and take it. When I reached for it he punched me in the face. Then he said he was going to kick my ass good and started punching me all over. Finally I took my pencil out of my pocket and threatened to stab him with it. Then the teacher got us and we were both sent home.'

Age 18–25: Non-violent self image

'I liked to gamble, mainly shoot dice. I was crazy about music. I could sing all of the songs by Johnnie Taylor and Al Green. I was also woman crazy. Women considered me a handsome cat. I wasn't Rudolph Valentino, but I was a nice-looking and smooth-talking dude. I knew how to handle broads who had any type of personality, but I dug best broads who were fun-loving but quiet and clean physically and mentally. All the broads that I messed with thought that I was a good lover. They all let me know that I had a big dick and that I knew how to use it. Every woman that I ever gave some to said that I was large-sized. But they thought that I was a nice dude to spend time with out of the bed too.

'The dudes that I ran around with knew that I got along good with the women. They considered me a player. They said that I was a pretty cool cat even though I was a country ass nigger. They also thought that I was a cat with a good voice who could sing blues just like Johnnie Taylor. They saw me win enough money to know that I could shoot dice good too.

'My people considered me a pretty fine young man who respected people older than him. They thought that I was a nice and courteous person. My father saw me as a young man trying to make it. He knew that I realized that I wasn't a child any more and that I had to make it on my own. He thought that I was man enough to take care of my own business and stay out of trouble.

'I liked to have fun, but I liked to avoid trouble and trouble-makers. I believed in respecting others, and I felt that I also deserved respect. I was a pleasant and good-humored dude. I tried to maintain a nice personality and a smile on my face. I could go for a joke. I didn't go around acting like any bad dude. I was a skinny ass motherfucker, and I knew that I had to be a little cool about fucking with people. The dudes that I ran around with thought that I was a good dude who was easy to get along with and so did the dudes that I worked with. I was a warm and free-hearted dude. I had feelings for people who were down and beaten. I'd do what I could to help a person. I'd share my last piece of bread with a hungry dude.'

Age 18–25: Negligible violent period

'I was mugged once but I never got into a fight where I jumped on somebody and shit.'

Escalating

The second type of career which violent actors have is escalating. An escalating career is where the self images and violent periods that an actor has had over his life have become more violent. Varying degrees of escalation were found among the actors with this type of career. Some actors had self images and violent periods which went from non-violent and negligible violent to incipient violent and unsubstantial violent and finally to violent and substantial violent. Other actors had self images and violent periods which went only from non-violent and negligible violent to incipient violent and unsubstantial violent. Case 34 illustrates the fully escalating career of a man who was convicted of aggravated assault.

Case 34, Age 12–16: Non-violent self image

'People saw me as the average school boy who loved sports and things. I especially liked basketball and my dream was to become the star player on the school team. Besides playing sports, I liked to build airplanes and talked about being an aeronautical engineer. My parents thought I was a good child. They liked it that I was heavy into aeronautics and sports. I didn't care about broads and running around. I was just content staying home around my family. The only thing that I ever did bad was stealing from my mother's pocketbook a couple of times. I guess I was what you would call a square kid.'

Age 12–16: Negligible violent period

'I never had any real fights then. Once I got into a shoving match with a kid, but this fight was so light that it's not really worth talking about. No hard punches were even thrown.'

Age 17–19: Incipient violent self image

'I was a square dude then, but I hated school and shoplifted. My good partners who were up to my game knew that I was a good thief. The broads and dudes at school saw me as pretty cool. They thought that I dressed sharp and talked fast. Although I was popular, a few people at school who I didn't mingle with thought I acted too uppity and had a smart mouth. Most people at school thought I was a slick dude, but I wasn't considered bad. They knew I'd slap a broad's face in a minute but I wouldn't jump on dudes.

'My steady woman saw me as a cool and popular dude. She thought I had good looks, good conversation, and good tastes. She figured that I was a dude who was going to be something. She dug everything about me except for my always running after other tail. My nose was always open for pussy. I chased the broads. When she got mad at me, she also called me a coward and said I would slap and hit broads, but I was scared to hit dudes. I admit it.

'My momma said that I was her baby and she spoiled me. But she was still pretty hip to my game. She figured I was doing some thieving and said I was sneaky. She also knew that I was a fiend behind pussy and wasn't satisfied with my steady woman's hole. She called me a nasty, dirty little bastard because I was always smelling after women's tails and catching the clap all the time. She was right too.'

Age 17–19: Unsubstantial violent period

Age 17–18: Unsubstantial violent acts 'I got into four or five heavy arguments with my steady old lady where I had to slap or punch her a few times. She was a big and solid-built broad and on two occasions I remember punching her once or twice in the face. On one of these occasions I busted open her lip and on the other I bruised her cheek up. That's about all I did to her. No police.'

Age 18: Unsubstantial violent act 'This broad at school was going around talking dirt about me. When I heard about it, I told her she better stop running off that shit to everybody, but she kept it up. So I ran her down after school one day and slapped her in the mouth. Then I tore her blouse off, shoved her down on the ground, and took off. Shit, she didn't get hurt, just embarrassed.'

Age 19: Unsubstantial violent act 'This broad who I was fucking on the side came over to my pad and said that she wanted to talk to my old lady about me. I told her to split but she wouldn't. When I started pushing her ass toward the front door, she put up a fight. So I hit the bitch with my fists in the face and bloodied her nose. Then my old lady ran into the room and jumped on the bitch too. As we pushed her out of the door, my old lady ripped her blouse off. No police.'

Age 20–28: Violent self image

'I was a simple pimp and dope fiend. I just wanted enough money so I could lay back, relax and stay high. I didn't want to work period. I figured that I would never have anything working at any eight hour a day job, but I could hustle women and make over a couple of hundred dollars a night. I wanted to have fine clothes and get a nice automobile the easy way. I considered myself a lover of women and was hung up behind getting new pussy. I thought that every foxy broad who walked down the street was a better fuck than the broads I had. I always had to check to see if they would dig on me. I was looking to be a big hustling pimp. People said that I had good looks, good conversation, and women enjoyed my company and that's all you needed to be a pimp. I was dreaming of the day when I would have five or six hos and could just kick back and let them take care of me.

'Street people, hustlers, dope peddlers, and other pimps considered me to be cool and accepted me as one of their own. They knew that I was no fool and gave me my respects. They knew if I had to get down I would, so I didn't have to worry about anybody bothering my women. I was scared to get down with a man with only my hands, but I wouldn't hesitate to with a gun or knife, or if I could pick up something. My two old ladies who were with me the longest were scared to death of me. I would beat a woman's ass twice as fast as a man's. They knew that I'd whip their asses good in a minute. Shit, I believed in beating women's asses. One of them was scared that I might ruin her one day. If I got into a mad state of mind, I could kill somebody. When I came down off dope, my old ladies watched themselves because I got mad quick. They knew that I only loved myself and didn't care about anybody else and that I was good to be with when things were going good but hell to be around otherwise. But they still wanted me for their husband.

'My people thought that I was doing what I pleased and trying to get everything that I possibly could from anybody, including them. They knew I was taking dope and hustling women. They said that I was no good to myself or anybody else. Shit, I didn't care what they said. I liked taking dope, hustling women, and acting bad. I enjoyed it all.'

Age 20–28: Substantial violent period

Age 20: Substantial violent act 'I was just hanging around outside of Tom's Bar one night when I spotted this fine built middle-aged broad walking down the street by herself. I started following her. Along the way I picked up a short board and when she passed by some empty garages, I fired on her. I busted her upside the head with the board and downed her. When I pulled her inside a garage, she started screaming so I beat on her with my fists until she promised to shut up. After I made her give me some head, I took her jewelry and money and split. No police.'

Age 21: Unsubstantial violent act   'One of my women and I drove around looking for broads who were hitchhiking. We picked up a couple of hippie chicks and pulled off on a lonely road. I slapped and backhanded them in the face and then we demanded all of their money. We searched both of them everywhere. We looked in their purses, pockets, bras, and panties. One of them tried holding out on us so I gave her a couple of hard shots in the breast and stomach. No police.'

Age 23: Substantial violent act   'I had won over $600 gambling in a game behind a bar I hung out at. When I headed home with the money, two of the dudes who were there started following me. I picked up a large stone and waited for them to make their play. When they fired on me, I hit one of the s.o.b.'s in the head with the stone and downed him. The other one then busted me in the head with a jack handle and took my money. I had to go to the hospital and get fifteen stitches. No police.'

Age 26: Substantial violent act   'This dude who I had dealt a little dope with latched onto one of my hos. I went over to his pad to talk to him about it to see what he had to say. We got into a heavy argument behind it and he said he was going to get his gun, so I knocked him down. Then I pulled out my knife and stuck him twice in the stomach. We started wrestling on the floor and I dropped my knife. When he got still, I noticed he was bleeding like a pig. I got scared he might die so I rushed him to the hospital after he promised not to put the police on me. I then backtracked to his pad to jump my ho for causing me all of this trouble. I punched her in the face until she fell down. Then I kicked the shit out of her all over the head and body. I broke her nose, jaw, and some of her ribs. No police.'

Age 27: Substantial violent act   'My old lady came home unexpectedly one day and caught me getting down with another broad. She started screaming at us and going crazy. I told the broad that she'd better split because I had to straighten that bitch out. As soon as she left, I jumped into my old lady's ass good. I punched her in the arms, back, and face and then I busted her head up against the wall five or six times. After that I just grabbed her ass by the shoulders and threw her right into the wall. She fell to the floor and I kicked her in the stomach until she doubled up. When I finally finished with her ass, she had to stay in the hospital for a few days. No police.'

Case 38 illustrates the partially escalating career of a man who was convicted of criminal homicide.

Case 38, Age 10–15: Non-violent self image

'I was slick for my age. I hung out with a gang of older dudes and cut school, played pool and ran away from home. I was also into stealing and got booked for it when I was ten. Stealing was an everyday thing for me then. I stole bikes, burglarized houses, and shoplifted whiskey and wine to sell to older dudes. I loved stealing. It was exciting, thrilling, and it gave me plenty of money to spend and made me pretty independent. All my friends thought I was doing good. They admired me for being a good thief. They knew that I could always get the goods and that I rarely got caught. I was known as such a good thief that older dudes in the neighborhood were always after me to steal something for them. They saw me just as a good thief.

'My family thought I was a bad delinquent. But I wasn't a for-real low rider or heavy gangster. I was into stealing and cutting school, not fighting. I just didn't dig school or my home. I disliked the authority of the teachers at school and of my father at home. I wanted to get away from all that shit that teachers said at school everyday and that my father was talking at home. I just didn't like adults in general and I felt that the whole world was against me and my friends.'

Age 10–15: Negligible violent period

Age 11: Unsubstantial violent act 'I got into an argument with another kid and he hit me with his skate in the arm. I got mad and bit his thumb. Neither one of us was really hurt.'

Age 16–19: Incipient violent self image

'I wanted to prove that I was a man, but I wasn't showy, and I didn't try to draw attention to myself. I was always quiet and never spoke just for the hell of it. I just didn't give a fuck and wanted to do what I wanted. I was real independent from my family. I acted like a low rider. I ran away from home and cut school, and I liked to smoke weed, drop LSD and shoot pool and talk about pussy. I also committed burglaries. I was a sneak thief, and I identified with the whole low rider trip.

'The squares at school considered me an outcast. They knew that I always cut school and got loaded and that I had gone to jail. They thought that I was the type of dude who didn't give a fuck about anything. They thought that I always was tense and looked mean. They were leery of me.

'My light and heavy partners considered me pretty cool and hip. They thought that I was all right, but too stubborn and bullheaded sometimes since I didn't like to take no for an answer. They all thought that I had a real hot temper because when I got mad, I'd threaten to kill people and shoot them and shit. But they didn't think that I would actually do it. They just knew that I was an explosive person, so you didn't fuck with me. My family thought that I was hot tempered too and irresponsible. They knew that I was a thief and a low rider.'

Age 16–19: Unsubstantial violent period

Age 16–18: Unsubstantial violent acts 'I used to slap my sister around good and plenty, but I didn't ever seriously injure her.'

Age 17: Unsubstantial violent act 'I was waiting at a bus stop next to some middle-aged man for the bus. When it came, he stepped in front of me and tried to get on the bus ahead of me, but I quickly jumped in front of him and stepped up onto the bus first. When I got to the top of the bus stairwell, he said some shit to me about pushing in front of him, and I turned around and told him, "Fuck you." He then started rushing up the steps of the bus door after me, so I kicked him hard in the chest twice and he fell down the steps of the bus. I then went to the back of the bus and sat down, and he got on the bus and started crying out to the bus driver. The bus driver said he wasn't getting into it, that it wasn't any of his business. Nothing else came down.'

Age 18: Unsubstantial violent act 'I got into a light fight at the pool hall. These two dudes were playing eight-ball, and I told one of them that I wanted to play a game or two, but he told me that I had to wait my turn like everybody else. I got mad because I didn't feel like waiting any longer, and I punched the dude hard in the mouth, but everybody rushed up and grabbed us right after I punched him, and that ended the fight. No police.'

Age 19: Unsubstantial violent act 'I was driving around in a friend's car when I saw this dude who I held a grudge against getting into a parked car. I was packing a .32, so I decided to shoot at him a few times and scare the fuck out of him. I slowed down beside his car and fired four shots at him and fucked up his car real bad. I got charged with doing it, but I wasn't convicted.'

Age 19: Unsubstantial violent act 'I was at a pool parlor in my neighborhood when this white social worker came in who was known as a snitch. I told him to get his white ass out of the place because we didn't dig him being around, but he wouldn't leave, so I finally swung the cue stick at him. He knocked the stick away with his arm and then walked out. I swung the stick at him hard, but I wasn't really trying to hit him. I just wanted to scare him good so he would get the fuck out of the place. No police.'

Age 19: Unsubstantial violent act 'I got into a fight with X behind him not paying me back some money that he owed me. When I asked him for the money, he said, "What money?" He outright denied that I ever loaned him any money. I got so mad that I felt like killing him. I pushed him down and kicked him a few good times. Then he suddenly remembered borrowing the money, and he told me that he would pay me some back soon, so everything was cool. No police.'

Case 45 illustrates another partially escalating career of a man who was convicted of criminal homicide.

Case 45, Age 14–18: Non-violent self image

'I was a nice guy who got along good at home and at school. I wasn't seen by my family or people at school as a goody-goody or a troublemaker. I was friends with people who were both. Nobody thought that I was tough, but they didn't think I was a chickenshit either.

'I made out o.k. in school. I tried hard and did about average in my studies and I was a good athlete. People at school considered me a hell of a track star. I didn't have to sit in the back seat to anybody as far as my looks were concerned. I let my hair grow out and with it long, the girls thought I was a real good-looking and cute dude. But I didn't take full advantage of it since I didn't have enough confidence in myself to act like a cool playboy. Secretly, I was a sensuous motherfucker. I wanted to date all the girls in school and fuck them too, but I just wasn't aggressive enough to meet them. I only expressed my personableness around the girls that I knew and had talked to or else who I heard dug on me.'

Age 14–18: Negligible violent period

Age 16: Unsubstantial violent act 'I took my steady girlfriend to a movie. Three guys came and sat near us. One of the guys who I knew said, "X, can't you do any better than that?" I ignored his remark at the time, but the next day I ran into him while I was caddying. I jammed him behind it and gave him a hard slap to the mouth. He didn't hit me back so I just said, "Don't ever pull that shit again" and walked off and that was the end of it. No police.'

Age 19–21: Non-violent self image

'I was a damn good salesman, and I was doing great at my job. In fact, I had about the best sales job in the whole company where I worked. I could sell just about anything. I was very personable, and I could talk that sales shit. I loved the selling contests that the company regularly had because I always finished near the top. I was getting a lot of confidence in my ability to earn a good living selling. My boss considered me the top dog salesman in the whole place since I always rolled in those sales. He thought that I was a together young man who was really going places. The other salespeople thought that I was doing good too. They saw me as a sharp salesman and as a ladies' man too. They were jealous because I made those commissions and got plenty of good pussy too. They knew that I had a stacked old lady and a cute little girlfriend on the side.

'I had the world by the ass then. I was making plenty of money, drove a Grand Prix, acted cool, and fucked hard too. I was a wet and

71

wild dude. I was hot in two beds, and I loved it. It was the best time of my life. I had my wife hanging on by her tits and had my girlfriend by her clit. My wife wanted to keep me, and my girlfriend wanted me to marry her.

'My girlfriend thought that I was too much. She knew that I had a lot of things going for me. She thought that I had a good job, dressed sharp, and was a goodlooking dude who acted cool. She even said that I was the hottest dude who ever laid her in a bed. My wife figured that I was living fast and wild, and she knew that I was playing around. She knew that I dressed way too sharp to be just going to work, and she was right. She thought I acted too cool and confident and arrogant. She called me a fingersnapper, a Casanova type who thinks he is a big cool lover. I liked to get down with her, but she was shy and got to be a boring homebody. I just told her that I was old enough to go to town when I pleased and do what I pleased, and I did too.'

Age 19–21: Negligible violent period

'I didn't have any real fights during this period. I got into arguments occasionally with my wife and girlfriend, but I never hit them.'

Age 22–24: Incipient violent self image

'As far as work was concerned, I was doing great. I had established myself a reputation for being an outstanding salesman. I knew I could land a selling job anywhere and easily earn a good living. But as far as my home life, it was fucked up bad. I got divorced from my first wife and married my girlfriend. She felt I was a good salesman who would always have a good paying job and she thought I could handle money well. She said I always dressed sharp, kept clean, and looked nice. I wasn't a slob and I got down with her good.

'But she also thought I was a fucked-up asshole so she divorced me. Right after we got married she lost her respect for me. She said that I was a boring, nosy, possessive person with a wild temper. She felt that I was a bore because I just wanted to make love to her all the time. And she thought that I was nosy and possessive because I always wanted to know what she was doing and who she was doing it with. But I felt that I had a right as her husband to know about this shit. She said it was just jealousy and she was scared where it might lead with my temper. I didn't go around blowing my temper every day, but I would get mad once in a while and smack her or threaten to beat the shit out of her to make her act right. She called me a woman hitter and said she hoped a dude would kick the shit out of me. Shit, I wasn't scared of dudes; I just didn't believe that a husband should put up with that crap from his wife.

'Her family, of course, agreed with her. They thought that I wasn't a man but a dog that only wanted to fuck, threaten and slap women around all day and sit on my ass. They resented me. But my family thought that I was a fool to put up with my second wife. They felt that she was going to do nothing but bring me trouble and that I better leave her. Shit, I was driven up the wall by her crap, but I wasn't able to cut her loose.'

Age 22–24: Unsubstantial violent period

Age 22: Unsubstantial violent act 'About 2.00 one morning I was in bed with my second wife when I got a horny nut. I woke her up, but she got indignant. I got mad because I really wanted to get down, so I slapped her in the face twice and shook her hard. She got mad at me, but it blew over quick. No police.'

Age 22: Unsubstantial violent act 'My second wife and I were driving to her parents' house on Christmas Day when we got into a heavy argument. I grabbed one of her arms and told her to shut up and she scratched me. Then I really got pissed at the bitch and pulled the car off the side of the road and grabbed her in a heavy headlock. I told her that she better listen to me, but she wouldn't. She kept scratching me and when I let her go, she ran out of the car. I chased down the crazy bitch, pushed her down and pulled her back to the car. She wasn't really hurt, but her ears were reddened up good from the headlock that I put on her. No police.'

Age 22: Unsubstantial violent act 'Right after I had told my second wife not to ever be going any place with other dudes, I discovered that she did it. I was mad that she wouldn't listen to me and I blew up. I started breaking everything in the house, the dishes, the clock, when I thought that I should get her and teach her dirty ass a lesson. So I punched her with my fists in the back two or three times and knocked the breath out of her. She threatened to call the police on me but never did.'

Age 23: Unsubstantial violent act 'After my second wife and I had separated, I heard that she had some dudes after me so I started packing a pistol. One night when I walked out of a steak and eggs house, this dude jammed me in the parking lot and said, "Aren't you X?" I said, "Yeah, that's me, but who are you?" He said, "I heard about you." I said, "Man, I don't know what the hell you are talking about." Then he downed me with a punch and started kicking me. I pulled out my pistol and told him to back off quick. When I headed toward my car, he said, "Fuck your gun, punk" and walked toward me. I cocked the trigger on my pistol and said, "If you take another step you dumb asshole, I mean it, I'll kill you." Then a friend of his said, "Stop, stop"and I got into my car and split. No police.'

Age 24: Unsubstantial violent act 'My second wife and I had been back together for about a week or so when we went to a pool party at our apartment building. I was drinking beer and having a mellow old time when I noticed her playing around with this single young dude. I told her to cut that crap out but later on I picked up on the body language that she was giving off to that dude. After I began watching her some more I noticed that she was giving him the eye too and the dude was tuned in on it. I tried to stay cool, but I felt that I shouldn't put up with that crap. She was living in my house and flirting with a dude like that right in front of me. That was it, I had had it with the dirty bitch. I took her in my apartment and asked her what the fuck she thought she was doing. I felt like she should get her ass kicked for doing that crap. I went into a rage and hit her with my fists twice in the ribs and pushed her down on the floor. Then I tore all the shades and shit down from the apartment and screamed at her. I didn't seriously injure her, but the next day she left me for good.'

De-escalating

A third type of career which violent actors may have is de-escalating. A de-escalating career is where the self images and violent periods that an actor has had over his life become less violent. The only actors who were found with this type of career were participant observation cases. In these cases, the self images and violent periods of the actor went from violent and substantial violent to incipient violent and unsubstantial violent and finally to non-violent and negligible violent. The fact that studies have shown that violent offenders are most frequently between the ages of fifteen and thirty[2] suggests that most violent actors have de-escalating careers. Participant observation case 2 below illustrates the de-escalating career of a man in his late thirties who earlier in his life was arrested for aggravated assault.

Participant Observation Case 2, Age 15–21: Violent self image

'I was the leader of X gang. I had a bad ass reputation. I did some of everything – joy ride in stolen cars, take hubcaps, shoplift whiskey and wine, crash parties, and run the streets chasing broads. I wasn't known as a heavy thief because I eased back off stealing the big stuff – the grand larceny raps. But I was known as one of the toughest dudes on – street. People around there knew that I was mean and liked to fight. I didn't mind fighting at all. Either you were ready to fight or you were a sissy punk who got kicked in the ass. I wasn't backing down or running off from anybody. Everybody knew that I would get down. I didn't believe in arguing with people; I'd push the button on them. I'd fire on them and be done with it. When I got uptight, I could explode. I would use my fists because I was fast and could box good, but I wasn't scared to use a knife, chain, gun, or anything else. I wasn't out to kill anybody, but if it had become necessary, I would have. I wanted to be a bad motherfucker and not take any shit. I admired dudes who could kick ass.'

Age 15–21: Substantial violent period

Age 15: Substantial violent act 'I had a job at a car wash on the weekends. One Saturday I got into an argument with this other dude working there. I got mad, threw a bucket of water on him, and then jumped on his ass. We started wrestling all over the floor and the other workers broke it up and told us to take it outside. When we got outside, we started throwing punches. Then I knocked him up against a wall and laid one punch after another on his face until the boss and other workers pulled me off him. The boss couldn't stop the blood coming from the top of both his eyes and they had to rush him to the emergency room where he got a dozen stitches. I was fired. No police.'

Age 16: Substantial violent act 'I was out for this dude's ass

75

because he had broken the screen door at my house. We had almost gotten down before behind this but it was broken up. Finally I heard he was at this party nearby and I went over there and called him outside. We got to boxing in the street and he tackled me. Finally I got back up and caught him with a hard punch which bloodied his nose and then another, but an even harder one which opened up his mouth. After that, he put his hands down and said he had enough. I said, "Fuck you giving up", and kept beating on him like a punching bag until I saw the police coming. His nose was broken, he got stitches in his lip and he lost a tooth. The police didn't catch up to me.'

Age 17: Substantial violent act   'My friends and I were out in front of the barbecue pit we hung out at when these dudes came by and said, "Motherfuckers, you better get the fuck out of here; if you don't, somebody's going to die." We shot back, "Eat it, punks." Then they said, "Motherfuckers, you're in trouble now" and started coming after us. We were carrying short swords that we had just stolen from the Masons and when we pulled them out, those dudes broke and ran. We chased their asses and I hit one of them over the head hard with my sword and dropped him. Blood was rushing out of the center of his head and we got scared and split. I hurt that fucker bad. An ambulance came for him. No police.'

Age 18: Substantial violent act   'My friends and I were at a park drinking whiskey and quarts of beer when we got into an argument with these other dudes who drove up. All hell broke loose. I grabbed onto this dude and he knocked me down and started choking me. Then I bit him in the thigh until I could taste his blood. He finally got my teeth out of him, but I got up and stomped him in the spine as hard as I could. Then the police drove up and everybody started running. I wasn't caught, but I hurt that dude bad. The police took him to the emergency room.'

Age 20: Substantial violent act   'My brother and I went to this party that a girl who lived behind us was giving. There were a lot of people there from other neighborhoods and it wasn't too long before trouble broke out. This dude came up to me and jammed me behind some dumb bullshit. I wanted to have a good time so I passed it off. Then he went up to a friend of mine and jammed him too. After that, he got back on my case. Finally I had had enough of the dude and told him to get out of my face or be ready to get down. He had a lot of partners at the party with him so I slipped back home and got my pistol. When I returned to the party, everybody was outside. I fired two shots over the heads of the dude who had jammed me and his partners and told them to get the fuck going fast. But one of them yelled that I only had a blank gun. Then I got mad because they acted like I was bullshitting. Shit, I was serious. I was ready to shoot their fucking asses. I decided first come first served. The first dude who took a step forward I shot. Nobody else pushed it so I took off. An ambulance picked up the dude I shot and I was later arrested and placed on probation for it.'

Age 22–28: Incipient violent self image

'I was just the Joe Doe family man. I was married and had kids. My wife thought that I was a responsible young husband who worked hard every day and took care of his business. Besides being too bossy, she considered me a good husband. She said that I was a hip dude because I liked to have fun and party. I had a high school education and worked hard, but I wasn't getting anywhere fast. I was nothing big, just a factory worker who was at the bottom of the plant. My friends around the neighborhood saw me as a young working married man who was into sports. Shit, my biggest kick was drinking whiskey and chasing it with beer. I was popular and out-going and had a lot of friends. I was on baseball and football teams and played alleyball and shit with the other dudes. I was a good team member and they thought I was one of the more decent athletes in the group.

'They considered me a pretty bad dude in general and so did the people around the plant. They knew that I could swell up real big and lay it out to people if they fucked with me. Once I got all mad, I'd tell a person, "I'll kick your goddamn ass if you don't back up." If I was really pushed hard behind something, I could get it on, but being married and having kids made me be slicker and wiser in dealing with people. I would put shit on them that I was going to do this and that, but not let it go. I tried to back them up without really getting it on.'

Age 22–28: Unsubstantial violent period

Age 23–24: Unsubstantial violent act   'A guy that I worked with at

the plant was always bugging me while I worked by arguing with me about this or that shit. I warned him to cut it out but he kept up this shit. Finally one day he took a potshot at me and said, "Why don't you just get your dumb fucking ass out of here?" I decided that I was going to set that dirty redneck straight. So I backhanded him across the face and said, "Don't ever fuck with me anymore." I also had to do this to another redneck around there for fucking with me too, about a year later. But I didn't injure either one of them bad or anything. No police.'

Age 26: Unsubstantial violent act 'My friend and I were at a football game and we made some bets with the guys sitting behind us. We were drinking and bullshitting them when an argument broke out near the end of the game. We told them that we were going to kick their asses and shit if they didn't pay up. Finally, out in the parking lot I pushed one of the dudes down and kicked him in the back. A policeman came up and broke it up but nobody was arrested. I don't think the dude I kicked was seriously hurt.'

Age 27: Unsubstantial violent act 'When I was walking out of the plant one day with my friends, this dude who I had just told to stop horsing around with me came up and gave me a play kick in the ass. It really humiliated me that he did that shit again right in front of my friends so I jumped that motherfucker. I grabbed him around the throat and choked him, but I eased up just before I really hurt him and said, "Please don't ever do that shit again to me." No police.'

Age 29–31: Incipient violent self image

'I was a divorcee. My wife and I got divorced because she wanted a full-time job and I wanted a wife who stayed home. After we separated, I got into running the streets and chasing women. I just wanted any woman who I could hit on for the night – nothing serious. My people thought I had an untogether social life dogging around after women all the time. But my friends thought I was a party man who always had a lot of fun.

'The clique that I was in at work thought I was a heavy rapper and politically hip. I became their representative to the union and management. They considered me a loyal leader because I didn't take any shit from management and I bitched like hell to the union. I had a reputation around the plant as a militant rabble rouser.

'People thought that I was a wild crazy dude but not bad. They knew I would put people in their place. If somebody rubbed my ass good, then I'd ruffle up like a choice rooster, throw a few bad words at them and act like I was going to step across their chest. But I'd only go so fucking far. I wasn't out to really get down unless I had to. Some people who knew me then said I got into people's asses too quick and they thought I should lighten up.'

Age 29–31: Unsubstantial violent period

Age 29: Unsubstantial violent acts 'I picked up a girl from a bar one night and brought her over to my apartment. We had some food, drank some wine. It was time for romance but she just backpedalled and announced she was leaving. So I said, "You filled your stomach with food, drank your fill and now you want to leave, right?" She said, "That's right, I'm leaving." Then I got pissed off at the dirty bitch and slapped her upside the head hard and knocked her down. Then I opened the door, kicked her in the butt and told her to get the fuck out. I had a few other similar incidents too, but I never really beat up any of the bitches. No police.'

Age 30: Unsubstantial violent act 'I was seeing this woman who was separated from her husband. I picked her up one night from her mother's house and she asked me where we were going. I told her to a little bar on X street. She got uptight and said, "I didn't get all dressed up for you to take me to some cheap bar." I said, "Well, that's all I can do tonight; I'll take you to a better place some other night." She said, "If that's all you can do, then I'm not about to give you any pussy tonight." I said, "If that's the way you want to be about it, I don't need you." She said, "Well, I didn't need you from the beginning." Then I really got mad and slapped her across the damn face. After I slapped her, she said, "Just take me home", so I did. When she opened the car door and started to get out, I kicked the dirty bitch in the ass. No police.'

Age 31: Unsubstantial violent act 'I was at a cabaret when I bumped into a guy and spilled my drink on his date. The guy said, "Hey, man, you spilled your liquor on my woman's dress." I said, "I'm sorry about that." Then he said, "Well, how about you paying to get her dress cleaned?" I said, "Look, it was an accident; I wish I had kept my liquor in my glass." He said, "I don't care what it was, you better give me the money to get her dress cleaned." I had had it with that fucking dude then. I shoved him hard and said, "Get fucked, if you want the money that bad, come on and get it." The other people came over and broke it up. No police.'

Age 32–38: Non-violent self image

'I have the top job at the plant where I work – a better job than any of the foremen. I'm the full-time union representative for the three hundred men at my shop. I'm their lawyer. I handle all of their problems on the job. They know I have power to move any foremen out of the shop who won't play ball and they respect me for it. I have a reputation as a bad committee man. Management and union people both see me as a progressive union man who is loyal to the union leadership. Union bosses consider me an up-and-coming committee man who can be groomed for high office. They know I'm a good bargainer and arbitrator and can organize men to follow me. I would say that I have a good future in the union.

'My friends at work think that I treat people as individuals and that I'm easy to get along with. They see me as a helpful and warm person who is not uptight. They know that I like to laugh and joke a lot and that I'm a big bullshitter. I can beat most people at it. I can really turn people around with the lines that I lay on them. I enjoy putting bullshit on people because it breaks up the monotony of the day and is a good break from the routine problems on the job.

'My second wife thinks that I'm a good husband except that I give too much of my time to my job and I'm occasionally flirty. But she knows that I'm basically a family-oriented man who is one hundred per cent loyal to her and the kids. I make my family's needs come first even though I like expensive cars and clothes and like to spend money. She knows that I can wear a lot of different caps around the house. I can cook, wash, clean, take care of babies and be a handyman. My mother and brothers see me as a steady type of individual who makes good money and is reliable and responsible. They think that I know where I'm going and don't get sidetracked. They are real proud of me.'

Age 32–38: Negligible violent period

'I have had some arguments but not anything close to fights with people during this time.'

8 Summary and conclusion

Several important findings emerged from this study of violent criminality. First, it was suggested that actors commit violent criminal acts *only after* they form violent interpretations of the situations which confront them. These violent interpretations of the situation fall into four types – physically defensive, frustrative, malefic, and frustrative-malefic. Secondly, it was found that whether or not actors actually carry out one of these violent interpretations of the situation is always *problematic*. It depends upon whether or not they stay in a fixed line of indication or form a restraining or overriding judgment. Actors commit violent criminal acts in the first and third cases, but in the second case, which is probably the most frequent, they do not. Thus, the violent interpretations which actors form have *variable* outcomes.

Thirdly, it was suggested that the self images of actors who commit violent criminal acts fall into three types – violent, incipient violent, and non-violent. Fourth, a linkage was found between the types of self images that actors hold and the types of interpretations they form of the situations in which they commit violent criminal acts. Actors who hold non-violent self images only commit violent criminal acts in situations in which they form physically defensive interpretations. Those holding incipient violent self images only commit violent criminal acts in situations in which they form physically defensive or frustrative-malefic interpretations. Finally, those holding violent self images commit violent criminal acts in situations in which they form physically defensive or any one of the three *offensive* interpretations. Thus, the type of self image that actors hold is crucially linked to the *range* and *character* of the situations that they interpret as calling for violence.

Finally, it was suggested that the careers of violent actors fall into three basic types – stable, escalating, and de-escalating. In stable careers, the types of self images the actors held over their lives and the kinds and amounts of violent acts they committed stayed fundamentally the same. In escalating careers, the types of self images the actors held over their lives became more violent as the kinds of violent acts they committed became more serious and the amount increased. In de-escalating careers, the types of self images the actors held over their lives became less violent as the kinds of violent acts they committed became less serious and decreased.

Two conclusions may be drawn from these findings. The first one is that persons who commit substantial violent acts have different generalized others (see Glaser, 1956; Hughes, 1962; Shibutani, 1955). Those who hold violent self images have an *unmitigated violent generalized other* – an 'other' which provides them with pronounced and categorical *moral* support for acting violently toward other persons. Those who hold incipient violent self images have a *mitigated violent generalized other* – an 'other' which provides them with pronounced, but *limited*, categorical moral support for acting violently toward other persons. Finally, those who hold non-violent self images have a *non-violent generalized other* – an 'other' which does not provide them with any pronounced, categorical moral support for acting violently toward other persons, *except* in the case of defending themselves or intimates from physical attack.

The second conclusion which may be drawn from these findings is that the generalized others of actors may change over time. Actors who have non-violent generalized others may develop mitigated and then unmitigated violent generalized others as in the case of escalating violent careers. As this takes place, these actors *expand* the range and character of the situations that they will interpret as calling for violence, commit more substantial violent acts, and eventually develop violent self images. Actors who have unmitigated violent generalized others may develop mitigated violent and then finally non-violent generalized others as in the case of de-escalating violent careers. As this takes place, these actors *constrain* the range and character of the situations that they will interpret as calling for violence, commit less substantial violent acts, and eventually develop non-violent self images.

The implication of this study is that the problem of violent crime centers around persons with violent generalized others. Not only do they commit the bulk of violent criminal acts, but they *victim precipitate* those which they do not commit. After forming offensive violent interpretations, they make physically threatening gestures toward persons with non-violent generalized others who as a result form physically defensive interpretations and then attack them. In this way, persons with violent generalized others are responsible for the violent criminal acts committed by persons with non-violent ones.

In short, violent generalized others play an important role in the formation of violent criminal acts. Thus, several questions need to be addressed in future research. First, to what extent, if at all, can the moral support for acting violently toward other persons provided by violent generalized others be codified into a specific set of norms or shared rules prescribing violent conduct? Second, regardless of the extent to which the moral support provided by violent generalized others can actually be codified into specific norms or shared rules, what is the nature of the social process which promotes their development among certain members of society? Finally, once developed, how can violent generalized others be transformed into non-violent ones?

Notes

1 A review and critique of the dominant approaches taken in the study of violent criminality

1 Studies done from the external pattern approach on other violent crimes include: Amir (1971), Bensing and Schroeder (1960), Chappell and Singer (1977), Curtis (1974), Driver (1961), Harlan (1950), Hepburn and Voss (1970), Landua *et al.* (1974), Levy *et al.* (1969), MacDonald (1971), Mulvihill *et al.* (1969), Pokorny (1965a, 1965b), Svalastoga (1962, 1956), Voss and Hepburn (1968), Wallace (1964), and Wolfgang (1958). For a critique of approaches like the external pattern one which rely upon official information for their source of data, see Kitsuse and Cicourel (1963).

2 Recent studies on violent criminality done from the personality approach include: Carrol and Fuller (1971), Fisher and Rivlin (1971), Fisher (1970), Justice and Birkman (1972), Lester *et al.* (1974), Lester and Perdue (1973), McCreary (1976), Mallory and Walker (1972), Megargee *et al.* (1967), Megargee and Cook (1967), Megargee and Mendelsohn (1962), Persons and Marks (1971), Perdue and Lester (1974, 1972), Rader (1977), Rawlings (1973), Sarbin *et al.* (1968), Sarbin and Wenk (1969), Wagner and Hawkins (1964), Warder (1969), and Wenk *et al.* (1968). For a critique of the use of this approach in the study of criminality, see Sutherland and Cressy (1978: 156–77).

3 They have discussed their application of this approach to the problem of violent criminality in a variety of places. See: Ferracuti and Newman (1974), Ferracuti and Wolfgang (1964, 1963), Wolfgang (1968, 1967), and Wolfgang and Ferracuti (1967a and 1967b). For other related studies of violent criminality done from the integrated approach, see: Ball-Rokeach (1973) and Ferracuti and Wolfgang (1973).

4 Although most studies of criminality and deviance are done from positivistic approaches, there have been some notable exceptions done from interpretative approaches. These include the studies done by Becker on marihuana use (1953), Cressey on the violation of financial trust (1953),

and Lindesmith on opiate addiction (1947). Douglas (1967) has provided an excellent, lengthy argument of the need for taking an interpretative approach in the study of suicide.

2 Symbolic interactionism: an interpretative approach

1 See especially Mead (1964: 243–7; 1936: 375–85, 401–4; 1934: 90–100, 117–35, 186–92) and Blumer (1969: 5, 12–16, 62–5, 72–3, 110–11; 1962: 181–3).
2 For discussions of the generalized other see: Mead (1964: 245–6; 1934: 62–3, 90, 152–64, 201–2, 265: 1932: 189–95), Blumer (1937: 180–4), Lindesmith et al. (1974. 166–7, 371–2), and Miller (1973: 51–6).
3 In an earlier paper (1974), I presented a preliminary analysis of the data obtained from this sample. A portion of the analysis of the entire sample appeared in a later paper (1977).

4 When interpretations of the situation lead to violent criminal acts

1 For other examples of actors who stayed in a fixed line of indication after forming other types of violent interpretations, refer back to the cases presented in Chapter 3.
2 It should be mentioned that there may be other types of reasons why actors form restraining judgments besides those which are presented here.
3 For additional examples of actors who overruled the restraining judgment that they made after forming a violent interpretation, see cases 57 and 29 presented in Chapter 6.

5 Self as object: self images

1 Typologies of violent offenders have been made on other bases besides their self images. Some recent examples are Cole, Fisher and Cole's typology (1968) of the 'personality styles' of 'murderesses,' i.e., masochistic, overtly hostile violent, covertly hostile violent, inadequate, psychotic, and amoral; Megargee's division (1966, 1965) of violent offenders into 'undercontrolled and overcontrolled personality types'; and Toch's typology (1969) of violence-prone personalities, i.e., self image promoting, self image defending, reputation defending, pressure removing, exploiting, bullying, self-defending, self-indulging, norm enforcing, and catharting. The common theoretical rationale underlying these typologies is that violent individuals always have some type of abnormal or deficient psychological makeup which causes them to commit violent criminal acts. The interpretations of situations made by them when they commit violent criminal acts are either totally ignored or treated as completely predetermined by their abnormal or deficient psychological makeups. Thus, this theoretical rationale is completely contrary to the one use here.

6 Self as object and process: the linkage between self images and interpretations

1 For another illustration of an actor with a violent self image and the malefic interpretation that he formed, refer back to case 35 in Chapter 3 and 5.

2 Likely exceptions might be provided by the professional or hired killer or actors who commit serious violent acts during riots. Unfortunately, no persons with these experiences could be found for interviews.

7 Careers of violent actors

1 In a paper describing findings from a national survey entitled 'Middle-Class Violence,' Stark and McEvoy report: 'The middle class is not only as likely as others ever to have engaged in physical aggression, but have done so as often. If anything, the middle class is more prone toward physical assault than the poor' (1970: 53). This finding may not be so startling considering that the questions used to measure 'interpersonal violence' failed to discriminate between unsubstantial and substantial acts of violence. The problems involved in deciding what is a violent crime are discussed briefly by Ferracuti and Newman in their review of 'assaultive offenses' (1974: 175–7).

2 This conclusion was drawn from a review of the findings on the ages of violent offenders provided in the following studies: Amir (1971), Bensing and Schroeder (1960), Chappell and Singer (1977), Mulvihill *et al*. (1969), Pokorny (1965a), Voss and Hepburn (1968), and Wolfgang (1958).

Appendix A
Data on convicted violent offenders

I. Source and selection of participants

The fifty-eight violent offenders whose interviews I used for this study came from five institutions in two states. Thirty-five of the offenders were inmates of four different institutions located in a far western state: a large county jail, a women's maximum security prison, and two men's maximum security prisons. The other twenty-three offenders were inmates of a men's maximum security prison located in a midwestern state. All told, forty-eight of the offenders were prison inmates and ten were jail inmates at the time of the interviews.

The violent offenders who I interviewed at these different institutions were in no sense randomly selected. No attempt was even made to select them in any standard way. My only concern was with finding offenders for interviews who had committed violent crimes in which they actually substantially injured someone. Thus, the main criteria that I used in selecting my cases was that the person was serving a sentence for a substantial violent crime. The initial 'formal' procedure that I used to contact such persons for interviews was to ask the prison or jail officials if I could examine their records in order to compile a list of inmates who fulfilled this criteria. This request was usually granted, or if not, the officials themselves compiled a list of violent offenders for me from an examination of their records. One institution which would not allow me to make such a list instead gave me a short list of the inmates who either volunteered in response to some of the treatment staff's announcement of the study in their therapy groups or who volunteered in response to an ad placed in the inmates' newspaper.

At any rate, I initially selected the inmates off whatever list I had at my disposal and asked them to participate in the study. Then I also tried to start up a friendship grapevine by asking the persons who I actually interviewed if they had any good friends who were serving sentences for violent crimes. If they did, I took their friends' names down and asked them to pass a good word to them about the study. Before I asked any of their friends to participate, I tried to check the official records to make sure they were actually serving a sentence for a substantial violent crime. At one institution a particularly influential inmate who participated in the study got six or seven of his associates who were serving sentences for substantial violent crimes to participate. I also tried to bump into as may inmates as possible in the prison, told them what I was doing, and asked them if they knew anybody who might be interested in participating in the study. If they did, I took their names down and tried to check the official records to see if they were serving a sentence for a substantial violent crime. If they were, I then asked them to participate in the study.

This was more or less the manner in which I contacted potential participants for the study. The much bigger problem, however, was getting offenders actually to participate, that is, get them to agree to be interviewed.

I usually saw the inmates privately and explained candidly to them what I was seeking to do. I told them I was a student and I was doing a study about people who commit violent crimes and how they came to commit them. I said that in order to get information on this, I wanted to interview persons who had actually committed violent acts and who would speak honestly about themselves and their violent experiences. Then I made it perfectly clear that I did not work for the Department of Corrections, the state, the police, etc., that I would keep all their remarks confidential, and that I would not provide any information on them to the correctional staff, other inmates, or anybody else. After explaining this, I asked if they had any questions, and they usually did. The most frequent ones were what was I getting out of doing the study; was I being paid to do it; if so, by whom; and how was it going to help them in the institution. I explained that carrying out a study was part of my graduate degree requirements and that their participation in it would not bear on their future in the institution one way or the other. Another question which often came up was whether I had a tape recorder in the office or in my briefcase, etc. I said 'no' and let them look in my briefcase, in the desk, and around the office.

After I answered all the questions, I emphasized that I only wanted to interview persons who would come out clean with the real facts about themselves and their experiences. Then I asked if they would be willing to help me out with the study and be interviewed for several hours. Some said they were not. For example, some people who were not interested said, 'No way I'm going to run down my crime and things I've done to you; shit, I wouldn't cop out on that to my own mother;' or 'Shit, I'm sorry I can't help you out, but like I'm innocent;' or 'Look, I'll tell you all you want to know about this fucking prison and the parole board or anything else, but I'm appealing my case and my lawyer told me not to discuss details with anybody'; or 'I'm just in here for fucking some bitch, not any for-real rape, so I don't righteously have any violent experiences to tell you about.' If the person seemed up-tight or was adamant, I just said, 'Well, thank you for your time,' and they left. But if they seemed fairly loose about it, I would say something like 'Ninety-nine per cent of the people in here say they're innocent, but I'm not interested in whether you should have been found legally guilty or not; I'm just interested in whether you did any violent thing.' Occasionally some who originally responded negatively would then agree to be interviewed.

On the other hand, some responded positively right off. For example, they said, 'Yeah, sure, I'll help you out; why not? It's not going to hurt me;' or 'O.K., I believe you; I'll do it;' or 'X said it was cool, so I guess I can go along with it;' or 'I'm game, let's get started.'

The fact that the persons who I interviewed were selected in a non-random and non-standardized fashion was of no consequence for my study. The conclusions which I sought to draw were not about the statistical distribution of characteristics of violent offenders or offenses, but rather were primarily about the social psychological processes at work in violent criminal acts. Thus, all that I was really concerned about was finding persons to interview who had actually committed substantial violent acts.

II. Conducting and validating the interviews

All the interviews with the offenders were conducted privately, and detailed notes were always taken during them. After each interview or some portion of it was completed, they were checked over, and anything that I didn't have time to write down during the interview was added. The questions always covered essentially the same set of topics with an important exception. The topics covered were: (1) the situation during which the actors committed the violent criminal act which led to their serving the sentence, (2) the situations in which they almost, but did not, commit violent acts, (3) the self images they held at the time of their offense, and (4) their violent careers, that is, their self image and violent act history. The exception was that I did not ask the persons at the institution in the midwest where I conducted my first set of interviews about the near violent situations which they may have had or their violent careers.

Further, I did not question every person who I interviewed in exactly the same way on each of these topics. Such a standarized technique would not have been fruitful since the persons who I interviewed came from a variety of cultural and social backgrounds. I usually tried to adjust the wording of the questions that I asked with this in mind. For example, I might ask with respect to the first topic, 'X, could you tell me in as much detail as possible how the situation occurred which led to your serving this sentence?' and later I would say, 'Now let's go back over this once more, and this time I want you to tell me what, if anything, you were thinking about and the order that you were thinking it as this situation unfolded.' Or I might ask with respect to this topic, 'X, could you run down to me in as much detail as possible what happened in the situation that led to you getting this beef?' Then later I would say, 'Now run this down once more, but this time tell me what, if anything, was on your mind and when it crossed your mind as this thing came down.' I continued to go over the same topic in this fashion until I felt that I had the facts down pat. Then I would turn to the next topic.

Many times after finishing a topic, the person I was interviewing wanted to engage in conversation unrelated to the study, for example, about sex on campus, what I did for entertainment, women's liberation, etc., so we often took short breaks to discuss such matters before moving on to the next topic. I conducted these interviews with the offenders in such a flexible and informal but systematic manner to help establish rapport with them. The degree to which this was done is evidenced, I believe, by the fact that seven inmates admitted during the interviews their forging of the violent crimes for which they had been sentenced though prior to that time they had consistently denied it (i.e., they had officially stated that they were innocent and doing time for a 'bum rap').

There was no way to validate all the information provided by the offenders during the interviews. The information which I could validate was that provided by the offender on the situation in which he committed the violent criminal act for which he was serving his present sentence and on his violent career. I validated the former by comparing his account of the situation in which he committed the violent criminal act with that found in the report of the incident made by the police. If the offender's description of the 'material facts' of the situation differed substantially from the one provided in the police report, then I discarded his entire interview. For example, if he reported that the victim was just a girlfriend of his who he went over to see but the police report indicated that the victim was a stranger whose apartment he forcibly entered, then his interview was thrown out. In most cases, the determination of the validity of the offender's account of the situation by this method proved fairly easy. Further, this method of validating the offender's account of the situation is more rigorous than it may perhaps appear. It is much more difficult than it may seem to falsify in a detailed and consistent manner the so-called 'subjective' side of a situation, that is, one's perceptions and evaluations, while at the same time not falsify any of its external or objective features. This, of course, is exactly what would have been needed in order for an offender to deliberately falsify this information and not have it detected by the validation procedure that I used.

The offender's account of his violent career could only be validated for the violent crimes for which he was at least officially charged. I did this by examining each offender's 'rap sheet,' that is, the list of all crimes for which an individual has been charged, with the date on which he was charged and the disposition of the charges (whether he was arrested, convicted, etc.). I compared the violent crimes noted on the offender's rap sheet with those that he described being officially charged with during the interview. If the offender's account of his official violent career did not correspond with that provided by his rap sheet, then I discarded his entire interview.

Further, for many of the offenders I was also able to examine more detailed police reports of past violent crimes for which they were arrested (jail inmates only) or convicted (prison inmates). If any of the offender's accounts of these past violent criminal acts differed substantially in terms of the material facts from the account provided in the police report, then I threw out the interview.

The validation methods just described were applied in a strict fashion. I did not, however, keep a count of the number of interviews which were discarded. The primary reason for this is that I tried not to complete interviews with persons who I suspected were deliberately falsifying information. Whenever I suspected that this was occurring during an interview, I would use a delaying tactic and then try to check the official records of the offender. For example, as soon as I finished covering the topic that we were on, I would say, 'X, I have an appointment that I forgot about, so we will have to get together later to finish this interview.' Many times I examined the offender's records beforehand. Then if he seemed to me beyond reasonable doubt to be falsifying information, I would say something like, 'O.K., X, thanks for your help, but I don't need any more cases like yours right now.' Incidentally, whenever I had to use either of these tactics, the offender never pursued finishing the interview but just left, so I suspect they knew that I was 'on' to them.

In my judgment, the data that were actually used in the analysis are very solid. The description of the offenders whose interviews were actually used in terms of their offense, sex, and approximate age at the time of the offence is presented below.

Description of the cases

Case No.	Convicted offense	Sex	Age
1	Criminal homicide	M	mid 20s
2	Criminal homicide	M	mid 20s
3	Criminal homicide	M	late 20s
4	Criminal homicide	M	mid 40s
5	Aggravated assault	M	late 20s
6	Aggravated assault	M	early 20s
7	Criminal homicide and forcible rape	M	mid teens
8	Criminal homicide	M	early 20s
9	Forcible rape	M	late 20s
10	Criminal homicide	M	late 20s
11	Criminal homicide	M	mid teens
12	Criminal homicide	M	early 30s
13	Criminal homicide	M	mid 30s
14	Forcible rape	M	early 20s
15	Forcible rape	M	late teens
16	Criminal homicide	M	early 30s

Case No.	Convicted offense	Sex	Age
17	Criminal homicide and robbery	M	mid 20s
18	Criminal homicide	M	mid 30s
19	Criminal homicide	M	late teens
20	Criminal homicide and robbery	M	mid 20s
21	Aggravated assault and robbery	M	early 20s
22	Criminal homicide	M	early 20s
23	Criminal homicide	M	late 40s
24	Aggravated assault and robbery	M	early 20s
25	Forcible rape and burglary	M	late 20s
26	Aggravated assault	M	early 20s
27	Aggravated assault	M	carly 30s
28	Criminal homicide	F	early 40s
29	Aggravated assault	F	early 30s
30	Criminal homicide	F	mid 30s
31	Aggravated assault	F	mid 20s
32	Aggravated assault	F	mid 20s
33	Aggravated assault	M	early 20s
34	Aggravated assault	M	late 20s
35	Aggravated assault	M	early 20s
36	Aggravated assault	F	late teens
37	Criminal homicide	M	mid 20s
38	Criminal homicide	M	late teens
39	Aggravated forcible rape	M	carly 20s
40	Forcible rape	M	late teens
41	Aggravated assault and robbery	M	mid 20s
42	Aggravated assault	M	early 20s
43	Forcible rape	M	early 20s
44	Aggravated assault	M	latc 20s
45	Criminal homicide	M	early 20s
46	Forcible rape	M	early 20s
47	Aggravated assault	F	mid 20s
48	Aggravated assault	F	early 20s
49	Forcible rape	M	late 20s
50	Aggravated assault	F	late 20s
51	Aggravated assault	F	early 20s
52	Criminal homicide	M	early 20s
53	Forcible rape*	F	late teens
54	Forcible rape	M	late teens
55	Criminal homicide	M	late teens

Case No.	Convicted offense	Sex	Age
56	Criminal homicide	M	early 30s
57	Criminal homicide	M	mid 30s
58	Criminal homicide	M	late 20s

*Sexual perversion with force.

Appendix B
Participant-observation of violent actors and acts

The participant observation that I drew upon in this research was at the time not done for the purpose of a study. In fact, I did this study as the result of my participant observation rather than the other way around. After observing many substantial violent acts and violent actors, I became interested in reading the formal literature on this topic during my first semester as a graduate student. Since I was struck by the fact that this literature did not correspond with my firsthand observations and experiences, I decided to carry out a study of my own on the problem of violent criminality.

My observations of substantial violent acts and experiences with violent actors date as far back as I can remember (about the time that I was in the third grade) and continued until sometime after I was a college student. Thus, it occurred for a period of well over ten years. I should point out, however, that during this period of time I only observed a couple dozen or so *substantial* violent acts and was well acquainted with less than a half dozen persons who I knew for a fact had and would commit such acts.

Nevertheless, I have observed substantial violent acts and actors of a variety of types. I have known violent actors who were old, as well as young and middle-aged. I have witnessed violent acts ranging from an attempted forcible rape to severe beatings to assaults with deadly weapons. The two most serious violent acts which I observed was a shooting and a stabbing in the eye with a can opener. In the attempted forcible rape, the victim was beaten and threatened with a broken bottle. I have also observed on separate occasions a person get smashed in the head with a brick, another hit in the head with a baseball bat, and dishes broken over a person's head. On several other occasions I observed fights where only hands and feet were used, but where bones were broken (cracked rib, broken nose or jaw) and where cuts were inflicted that required stitches. I also saw several severe chokings and many fistfights in which the persons involved were not substantially physically injured. The perpetrators and victims were in a few instances intimates, in several others neighbors and good acquaintances, and on a couple of occasions complete strangers. Sometimes the police became involved in these incidents, but usually they did not. The incidents were not localized in any specific spatial area. Some occurred in fields, parking lots, bars, others in cars, one in a gym downtown, some on my block, and a few around schools.

Besides stimulating my initial interest in studying violent acts, my observations and experiences played two crucial roles in the analysis that I carried out here. First, it provided me with many valuable hunches with which to build the analytical categories that I used in the study. Secondly, it provided me with an additional source of data against which to check the findings and conclusions of my study. This was particularly crucial since the main source of data used in the analysis came from interviews with convicted violent offenders. For example, I asked myself if all the actors that I had known well and had seen commit substantial violent criminal acts which were not victim-precipitated actually held violent or incipient violent self images; and, if so, if they had stable, escalating or de-escalating careers. After this study was initiated, I was also able to directly gather data on a couple of the actors who I knew for sure had or were still perpetrating substantial violent acts and used this as well in my analysis. This data proved to be especially helpful in the discovery of the de-escalating type of career since none of the convicted violent offenders had careers of this type. In short, my participant-observation of violent actors and acts played an important role in all stages of this study, i.e., in its inception, in the analysis of the data, and in drawing conclusions.

Bibliography

ABRAHAMSEN, D. (1960), *The Psychology of Crime*, New York: Columbia University Press.

AMIR, M. (1971), *Patterns in Forcible Rape*, Chicago: University of Chicago Press.

ATHENS, L. (1977), 'Violent Crime: A Symbolic Interactionist Study,' *Symbolic Interaction*, 1, Fall: 56–70.

ATHENS, L. (1974), 'The Self and the Violent Criminal Act,' *Urban Life and Culture*, 3, April: 98–112.

BALL-ROKEACH, S. (1973), 'Values and Violence: A Test of the Sub-culture of Violence Thesis,' *American Sociological Review*, 38, December: 736–49.

BANAY, R. (1952), 'Study in Murder,' *The Annals of the American Academy of Political and Social Science*, 284, November: 26–34.

BECKER, H. (1953), 'Becoming a Marihuana User,' *American Journal of Sociology*, 59, November: 235–42.

BENSING, R. and O. SCHROEDER, JR. (1960), *Homicide in an Urban Community*, Springfield: Charles Thomas.

BLUMER, H. (1975), 'Symbolic Interaction and the Idea of Social System,' Working paper, Berkeley: University of California.

BLUMER, H. (1969), *Symbolic Interactionism: Perspective and Method*, Englewood Cliffs: Prentice-Hall.

BLUMER, H. (1962), 'Society as Symbolic Interaction,' pp. 179–92 in A. Rose (ed.), *Human Behavior and Social Processes*, Boston: Houghton Mifflin.

BLUMER, H. (1937), 'Social Psychology,' pp. 148–98 in E. M. Schmidt (ed.), *Man and Society*, Englewood Cliffs: Prentice-Hall.

CARROL, J. and G. FULLER (1971), 'An MMPI Comparison of Three Groups of Criminals,' *Journal of Clinical Psychology*, 27: 240–2.

CHAPPELL, D. and S. SINGER (1977), 'Rape in New York City: A Study of Material in the Police Files and Its Meaning,' pp. 245–71 in D. Chappell, R. Geis, and G. Geis (eds.), *Forcible Rape: The Crime, the Victim, and the Offender*, New York: Columbia University Press.

BIBLIOGRAPHY

COLE, K., G. FISHER, and S. COLE (1968), 'Women Who Kill: A Socio-psychological Study,' *Archives of General Psychiatry*, 19, July: 1–8.

COOLEY, C. (1926), 'The Roots of Social Knowledge,' *American Journal of Sociology*, 32, July: 59–79.

CRESSEY, D. (1953), *Other People's Money*, New York: The Free Press.

CURTIS, L. (1974), *Criminal Violence*, Lexington: D. C. Heath.

DEUTSCHER, I. (1970), 'Buchenwald, Mai Lai, and Charles Van Doren: Social Psychology as Explanation,' *The Sociological Quarterly*, 11: 533–40.

DOUGLAS, J. (1967), *The Social Meanings of Suicide*, Princeton: Princeton University Press.

DRIVER, E. (1961), 'Interaction and Criminal Homicide in India,' *Social Forces*, 40, December: 153–8.

FERRACUTI, F. and G. NEWMAN (1974), 'Assaultive Offenses,' pp. 175–207 in D. Glaser (ed.), *Handbook of Criminology*, Chicago: Rand McNally.

FERRACUTI, F. and M. WOLFGANG (1973), *Psychological Testing of the Subculture of Violence*, Rome: Bulzoni.

FERRACUTI, F., R. LAZZARI, and M. WOLFGANG (1970), *Violence in Sardinia*, Rome: Bulzoni.

FERRACUTI, F. and M. WOLFGANG (1964), 'The Prediction of Violent Behavior,' *Corrective Psychiatry and Journal of Social Therapy*, 10: 289–301.

FERRACUTI, F. and M. WOLFGANG (1963), 'Design for a Proposed Study of Violence,' *British Journal of Criminology*, 3, April: 377–88.

FISHER, G. (1970), 'Discriminating Violence Emanating from Over-controlled versus Under-controlled Aggressivity,' *British Journal of Social and Clinical Psychology*, 9: 54–9.

FISHER, G. and E. RIVLIN (1971), 'Psychological Needs of Rapists,' *British Journal of Criminology*, 11: 182–5.

GLASER, D. (1956), 'Criminality Theories and Behavioral Images,' *American Journal of Sociology*, 61, March: 433–44.

HARLAN, H. (1950), 'Five Hundred Homicides,' *Journal of Criminal Law and Criminology*, 40, March–April: 736–52.

HARTUNG, F. (1966), *Crime, Law and Society*, Detroit: Wayne State University Press.

HEPBURN, J. and H. VOSS (1970), 'Patterns of Criminal Homicide: A Comparison of Chicago and Philadelphia,' *Criminology*, 8, May: 21–45.

HUGHES, E. (1962), 'What Other?,' pp. 119–27 in A. Rose (ed.), *Human Behavior and Social Processes*, Boston: Houghton Mifflin.

JEFFERY, C. (1960), 'The Historical Development of Criminology,' pp. 364–94 in H. Mannheim (ed.), *Pioneers in Criminology*, Chicago: Quadrangle Books.

JUSTICE, B. and R. BIRKMAN (1972), 'An Effort to Distinguish the Violent from the Nonviolent,' *Southern Medical Journal*, 65, June: 703–6.

KITSUSE, J. and A. CICOUREL (1963), 'A Note on the Uses of Official Statistics,' *Social Problems*, 12: 131–9.

LANDAU, S., I. DRAPKIN, and S. ARAD (1974), 'Homicide Victims and

Offenders: An Israeli Study,' *Journal of Criminal Law and Criminology*, 65, September: 390–6.

LESTER, D. and G. LESTER (1975), *Crime of Passion: Murder and Murderer*, Chicago: Nelson-Hall.

LESTER, D., W. PERDUE, and D. BROOKHART (1974), 'Murder and the Control of Aggression,' *Psychological Reports*, 34: 706.

LESTER, D. and W. PERDUE (1973), 'Movement Responses of Murderers to Rorschach Stimuli,' *Perceptual and Motor Skills*, 37, October: 668.

LEVY, J., S. KUNITZ, and M. EVERETT (1969), 'Navajo Criminal Homicide,' *South Western Journal of Anthropology*, 25, Summer: 124–52.

LINDESMITH, A. (1947), *Opiate Addiction*, Bloomington: Principia.

LINDESMITH, A., A. STRAUSS, and N. DENZIN (1974), *Social Psychology*, Hinsdale: Dryden.

McCREARY, C. (1976), 'Trait and Type Differences among Male and Female Assaultive and Non-Assaultive Offenders,' *Journal of Personality Assessment*, 40, December: 617–21.

MacDONALD, J. (1971), *Rape: Offenders and Their Victims*, Springfield: Charles Thomas.

MALLORY, C. and C. WALKER (1972), 'MMPI O-H Scale Responses of Assaultive and Nonassaultive Prisoners and Associated Life History Variables,' *Educational and Psychological Measurement*, 32: 1125–8.

MATZA, D. (1964), *Delinquency and Drift*, New York: John Wiley and Sons.

MEAD, G. H. (1964), *Selected Writings*, edited by A. Reck, Indianapolis: Bobbs-Merrill.

MEAD, G. H. (1938), *The Philosophy of the Act*, Chicago: University of Chicago Press.

MEAD, G. H. (1936), *Movements of Thought in the Nineteenth Century*, Chicago: University of Chicago Press.

MEAD, G. H. (1934), *Mind, Self and Society*, Chicago: University of Chicago Press.

MEAD, G. H. (1932), *The Philosophy of the Present*, LaSalle: Open-Court.

MEGARGEE, E. (1973), 'Recent Research on Overcontrolled and Undercontrolled Personality Patterns Among Violent Offenders,' *Sociological Symposium*, 9: 37–50.

MEGARGEE, E. (1966), 'Undercontrolled and Overcontrolled Personality Types in Extreme Antisocial Aggression,' *Psychological Monographs: General and Applied*, 80: 1–29.

MEGARGEE, E. (1965), 'Assault With Intent to Kill,' *Transaction*, 2, September–October: 27–31.

MEGARGEE, E. and P. COOK (1967), 'The Relation of T.A.T. and Inkblot Aggressive Content Scales With Each Other and With Criteria of Overt Aggressiveness in Juvenile Delinquents,' *Journal of Projective Techniques and Personality Assessment*, 31: 48–60.

MEGARGEE, E., P. COOK, and G. MENDELSOHN (1967), 'Development and Validation of an MMPI Scale of Assaultiveness in Overcontrolled Individuals,' *Journal of Abnormal Psychology*, 72: 519–23.

MEGARGEE, E. and G. MENDELSOHN (1962), 'A Cross-Validation of

Twelve MMPI Indices of Hostility and Control,' *Journal of Abnormal and Social Psychology*, 65: 431–8.

MILLER, D. (1973); *George Herbert Mead: Self, Language and the World*, Austin: University of Texas Press.

MULVIHILL, D., M. TUMIN with L. CURTIS (1969), *Crimes of Violence* (A Staff Report to the National Commission on the Causes and Prevention of Violence), vol. 11, Washington, D.C.: U.S. Government Printing Office.

PERDUE, W. and D. LESTER (1974), 'Racial Differences in the Personality of Murderers,' *Perceptual and Motor Skills*, 38: 726.

PERDUE, W. and D. LESTER (1972), 'Personality Characteristics of Rapists,' *Perceptual and Motor Skills*, 35: 514.

PERSONS, R. and P. MARKS (1971), 'The Violent 4-3 MMPI Personality Type,' *Journal of Consulting and Clinical Psychology*, 36: 189–96.

PITTMAN, D. and W. HANDY (1964), 'Patterns in Criminal Aggravated Assault,' *Journal of Criminal Law, Criminology and Police Science*, 55, December: 462–70.

POKORNY, A. (1965a), 'A Comparison of Homicides in Two Cities,' *Journal of Criminal Law, Criminology and Police Science*, 56, December: 479–87.

POKORNY, A. (1965b), 'Human Violence: A Comparison of Homicide, Aggravated Assault, Suicide and Attempted Suicide,' *Journal of Criminal Law, Criminology and Police Science*, 56, December: 488–97.

RADER, C. (1977), 'MMPI Profile Types of Exposers, Rapists, and Assaulters in a Court Services Population,' *Journal of Consulting and Clinical Psychology*, 45: 61–9.

RAWLINGS, M. (1973), 'Self-Control and Interpersonal Violence: A Study of Scottish Adolescent Male Severe Offenders,' *Criminology*, 11, May: 23–48.

SARBIN, T. and E. WENK (1969), 'Resolution of Binocular Rivalry as a Means of Identifying Violence-Prone Offenders,' *Journal of Criminal Law, Criminology and Police Science*, 60, September: 345–50.

SARBIN, T., E. WENK, and D. SHERWOOD (1968), 'An Effort to Identify Assault-Prone Offenders,' *Journal of Research in Crime and Delinquency*, 5: 66–71.

SCHUTZ, A. (1954), 'Concept and Theory Formation in the Social Sciences,' *Journal of Philosophy*, 51, April: 257–73.

SHIBUTANI, T. (1955), 'Reference Groups as Perspectives,' *American Journal of Sociology*, 60, May: 562–9.

STARK, R. and J. McEVOY, III (1970), 'Middle-Class Violence,' *Psychology Today*, 4, November: 52–4, 110–12.

SUTHERLAND, E. and D. CRESSEY (1978), *Criminology*, Philadelphia: Lippincott.

SVALASTOGA, K. (1962), 'Rape and Social Structure,' *Pacific Sociological Review*, 5, Spring: 48–53.

SVALASTOGA, K. (1956), 'Homicide and Social Contact in Denmark,' *American Journal of Sociology*, 62, July: 37–41.

TANAY, E. (1972), 'Psychiatric Aspects of Homicide Prevention,' *American Journal of Psychiatry*, 128, January: 49–52.

TAYLOR, I., P. WALTON, and J. YOUNG (1973), *The New Criminology: For a Social Theory of Deviance*, New York: Harper & Row.

TOCH, H. (1969), *Violent Men: An Inquiry into the Psychology of Violence*, Chicago: Aldine.

VOLD, G. (1958), *Theoretical Criminology*, New York: Oxford University Press.

VOSS, H. and J. HEPBURN (1968), 'Patterns of Criminal Homicide in Chicago,' *Journal of Criminal Law, Criminology and Police Science*, 59, December: 499–508.

WAGNER, E. and R. HAWKINS (1964), 'Differentiation of Assaultive Delinquents with the Hand Test,' *Journal of Projective Techniques and Personality Assessment*, 28: 363–5.

WALLACE, S. (1964), 'Patterns of Violence in San Juan,' pp. 43–8 in *Interdisciplinary Problems in Criminology: Papers of the American Society of Criminology*, Columbus: Ohio State University Publication.

WARDER, J. (1969), 'Two Studies of Violent Offenders,' *British Journal of Criminology*, 9, October: 389–93.

WENK, E., T. SARBIN, and D. SHERWOOD (1968), 'The Resolution of Binocular Rivalry among Assaultive and Nonassaultive Youthful Offenders,' *Journal of Research in Crime and Delinquency*, 5: 134–47.

WINCH, P. (1958), *The Idea of a Social Science*, London: Routledge & Kegan Paul.

WOLFGANG, M. (1969), 'Who Kills Whom,' *Psychology Today*, 3, October: 54–6, 72, 74–5.

WOLFGANG, M. (1968), 'Homicide,' pp. 490–5 in D. Sills (ed.), *International Encyclopedia of the Social Sciences*, vol. 3, New York: Macmillan and The Free Press.

WOLFGANG, M. (1967), 'Criminal Homicide and the Subculture of Violence,' pp. 3–12 in M. Wolfgang (ed.), *Studies in Homicide*, New York: Harper & Row.

WOLFGANG, M. (1958), *Patterns of Criminal Homicide*, Philadelphia: University of Pennsylvania Press.

WOLFGANG, M. (1957), 'Victim-precipitated Criminal Homicide,' *Journal of Criminal Law, Criminology and Police Science*, 48, June: 1–11.

WOLFGANG, M. and F. FERRACUTI (1967a), *The Subculture of Violence: Towards an Integrated Theory in Criminology*, London: Tavistock.

WOLFGANG, M. and F. FERRACUTI (1967b), 'Subculture of Violence – A Social Psychological Theory,' pp. 271–80 in M. Wolfgang (ed.), *Studies in Homicide*, New York: Harper & Row.

ZNANIECKI, F. (1968), *The Method of Sociology*, New York: Octagon Books.

Index

abnormal personality or psychological make-up, 4, 85

aggravated assault, cases of, 25, 26–7, 29–30, 36–8, 49

antecedent factors, 11–14

careers of violent actors, 52–80; de-escalating, 74–80, 82; escalating, 63–74, 82; and generalized other, 82; stable, 54–63, 82; types of, 54

criminal homicide, cases of, 21, 24, 30–1, 47–8, 56–8

de-escalating careers, 74–80; discovery of, 96; and generalized other, 82

description of study, 17–18, 87–96

escalating careers, 63–74; fully, 64–8; and generalized other, 82; partially, 68–74

External pattern approach: assumptions of, 1; critique, 11–14; illustration, 1–4; studies using, 84

fixed line of indication, 29–31, 38, 81; examples of, 29–31, 85

forcible rape, cases of, 23–4, 35–6, 50–1

frustrative interpretation, 22–4, 51, 81; examples of, 23, 24, 32–3, 35–6, 49–51

frustrative-malefic interpretation, 26–7, 51, 81; examples of, 27, 33–4, 37–8, 47–8

generalized other: and change over time, 17, 82; and self as object, 16–17; and self as process, 15–16; types of,

82; and violent interpretations, 19, 82

human action, as situated conduct, 12, 14

human being, as actor versus passive agent, 13–14

incipient violent self images, 42, 45, 51, 53, 64, 74, 81, 82, 96; examples of, 43, 46–7, 64–5, 69, 72–3, 77, 78–9

integrated approach: assumptions of, 8; critique, 11–14; illustration, 8–11; studies using, 84

interpretation of situation, as creative or formative process, 12; import of, 12–14; phases of, 15–16; and violent criminal acts, 19

interpretative approach: basic requirement of, 14; studies using, 84–5; and symbolic interactionism, 14–15

interviews with violent offenders: description of, 17, 88–90; means of validation, 91–2

malefic interpretation, 24–5, 51, 81; examples of, 25–6, 29–30, 31–2, 34–5, 36–7, 49

mitigated violent generalized other, 82

negligible violent periods, 53, 54, 64, 75; examples of, 62, 63, 64, 68, 71, 72, 80

non-violent generalized other, 82

non-violent self images, 43, 45, 51, 53, 64, 75, 81, 82; examples of, 43–4, 46, 61, 62–3, 64, 68, 70, 71–2, 80

103

Index

overriding judgment, 36, 38, 81; examples of, 36, 37–8, 47–8, 49

participant-observation: cases in text, 41–2, 75–80; description of, 95–6

personality approach: assumptions of, 4; critique, 11–14, 85; illustration, 4–8; studies using, 84

physically defensive interpretation, 20–1, 51, 81, 83; examples of, 21, 30–1, 46; and victim-precipitation, 21–2, 83

positivism: and approaches to violent crime, 11; definition of, 11; shortcomings, 11–14

restraining judgments, 31–6, 38, 81; from alteration of victim's conduct, 32–3; out of deference to another, 34–5; for fear of being unsuccessful, 31–2; for fear of damaging social relationship, 33–4; for fear of legal sanction, 35–6

self, basic aspects of, 15; as object, 16–17; as process, 15–16; relation of self as process to object, 17

self images, correlation to violent periods of life, 53–4, 82; and de-escalating careers, 74–5, 82; and escalating careers, 63–4, 82; formation of, 16–17; incipient violent, 42–3, 81, 82; non-violent, 43–4, 81, 82; relationships to violent interpretations, 45–51, 81–2; and stable careers, 54, 82; types of, 39–44, 53, 81; violent, 39–42, 81, 82

stable careers, 54–63, 82; non-violent, 61–3; violent, 54–61

subculture of violence hypothesis, description of, 8–9; Sardinian study of, 9–11

substantial violent acts, 17–18, 53, 54, 87, 89, 95, 96; examples of, 55, 56, 57, 58–9, 59, 60, 61, 66, 67, 68, 75, 76, 77

substantial violent periods, 53, 54, 64, 74; examples of, 55, 56, 57, 58–60, 61, 66–8, 75–7

typologies of violent criminals, 85

under- and overcontrolled personality hypothesis: description of, 4–6; study testing, 6–8

unmitigated violent generalized other, 82

unsubstantial violent acts, 53, 54; examples of, 59, 62, 65, 67, 69, 70, 71, 73, 74, 77, 78, 79–80

unsubstantial violent periods, 53, 54, 64, 74; examples of, 65, 69–70, 73–4, 77–8, 79–80

victim-precipitation, 53, 83; critique of behavioristic conception, 21–2; as physically defensive interpretation, 21

violent criminal acts: conscious versus unconscious conceptions of, 19–20; substantial, unsubstantial dichotomy, 53, 86

violent criminality: definition of, 1

violent generalized other: and norms, 83; and problem of violent criminality, 83; types of, 82

violent interpretations: and generalized other, 19, 82; and fixed line of indication, 29–31, 81; formation of, 19; frustrative, 22–4, 81; frustrative-malefic, 26–7, 81; malefic, 24–6, 81; and overriding judgment, 36–8, 81; physically defensive, 20–2, 81, 83; relationship to self images, 45–51, 81–2; and restraining judgments, 31–6, 81; types of, 20–7, 81; variable outcomes, 81

violent offenders in study: description of, 17–18, 92–4; means of selection, 87–9; source of, 17, 87;

violent periods of life, 54, 63–4, 74–5; correlation to self images, 53–4; types of, 53

violent self images, 39, 45, 51, 53, 54, 64, 74, 81, 82, 96; examples of, 39–40, 41–2, 48–9, 50–1, 54–5, 58, 60–1, 65–6, 75

violent situations: study of, 19–38; comparison of completed violent and near violent situations, 28–9, 38

Routledge Social Science Series

Routledge & Kegan Paul   London, Henley and Boston

39 Store Street, London WC1E 7DD
Broadway House, Newtown Road,
Henley-on-Thames, Oxon RG9 1EN
9 Park Street, Boston, Mass. 02108

Contents

Authors wishing to submit manuscripts for any series in
this catalogue should send them to the Social Science Editor,
Routledge & Kegan Paul Ltd, 39 Store Street,
London WC1E 7DD

●*Books so marked are available in paperback*
All books are in Metric Demy 8vo format (216 × 138mm approx.)

International Library of Sociology

General Editor   John Rex

GENERAL SOCIOLOGY

Barnsley, J. H. The Social Reality of Ethics. *464 pp.*
Brown, Robert. Explanation in Social Science. *208 pp.*
● Rules and Laws in Sociology. *192 pp.*
Bruford, W. H. Chekhov and His Russia. *A Sociological Study. 244 pp.*
Burton, F. and **Carlen, P.** Official Discourse. *On Discourse Analysis, Government Publications, Ideology. About 140 pp.*
Cain, Maureen E. Society and the Policeman's Role. *326 pp.*
●**Fletcher, Colin.** Beneath the Surface. *An Account of Three Styles of Sociological Research. 221 pp.*
Gibson, Quentin. The Logic of Social Enquiry. *240 pp.*
Glucksmann, M. Structuralist Analysis in Contemporary Social Thought. *212 pp.*
Gurvitch, Georges. Sociology of Law. *Foreword by Roscoe Pound. 264 pp.*
Hinkle, R. Founding Theory of American Sociology 1883-1915. *About 350 pp.*
Homans, George C. Sentiments and Activities. *336 pp.*
Johnson, Harry M. Sociology: *a Systematic Introduction. Foreword by Robert K. Merton. 710 pp.*
●**Keat, Russell** and **Urry, John.** Social Theory as Science. *278 pp.*
Mannheim, Karl. Essays on Sociology and Social Psychology. *Edited by Paul Keckskemeti. With Editorial Note by Adolph Lowe. 344 pp.*
Martindale, Don. The Nature and Types of Sociological Theory. *292 pp.*
●**Maus, Heinz.** A Short History of Sociology. *234 pp.*
Myrdal, Gunnar. Value in Social Theory: *A Collection of Essays on Methodology. Edited by Paul Streeten. 332 pp.*
Ogburn, William F. and **Nimkoff, Meyer F.** A Handbook of Sociology. *Preface by Karl Mannheim. 656 pp. 46 figures. 35 tables.*
Parsons, Talcott, and **Smelser, Neil J.** Economy and Society: *A Study in the Integration of Economic and Social Theory. 362 pp.*
Podgórecki, Adam. Practical Social Sciences. *About 200 pp.*
Raffel, S. Matters of Fact. *A Sociological Inquiry. 152 pp.*
●**Rex, John.** (Ed.) Approaches to Sociology. *Contributions by Peter Abell,* Sociology and the Demystification of the Modern World. *282 pp.*
●**Rex, John** (Ed.) Approaches to Sociology. *Contributions by Peter Abell, Frank Bechhofer, Basil Bernstein, Ronald Fletcher, David Frisby, Miriam Glucksmann, Peter Lassman, Herminio Martins, John Rex, Roland Robertson, John Westergaard and Jock Young. 302 pp.*
Rigby, A. Alternative Realities. *352 pp.*
Roche, M. Phenomenology, Language and the Social Sciences. *374 pp.*
Sahay, A. Sociological Analysis. *220 pp.*

Strasser, Hermann. The Normative Structure of Sociology. *Conservative and Emancipatory Themes in Social Thought. About 340 pp.*
Strong, P. Ceremonial Order of the Clinic. *About 250 pp.*
Urry, John. Reference Groups and the Theory of Revolution. *244 pp.*
Weinberg, E. Development of Sociology in the Soviet Union. *173 pp.*

FOREIGN CLASSICS OF SOCIOLOGY

● **Gerth, H. H.** and **Mills, C. Wright.** From Max Weber: *Essays in Sociology. 502 pp.*
● **Tönnies, Ferdinand.** Community and Association. *(Gemeinschaft and Gesellschaft.) Translated and Supplemented by Charles P. Loomis. Foreword by Pitirim A. Sorokin. 334 pp.*

SOCIAL STRUCTURE

Andreski, Stanislav. Military Organization and Society. *Foreword by Professor A. R. Radcliffe-Brown. 226 pp. 1 folder.*
Carlton, Eric. Ideology and Social Order. *Foreword by Professor Philip Abrahams. About 320 pp.*
Coontz, Sydney H. Population Theories and the Economic Interpretation. *202 pp.*
Coser, Lewis. The Functions of Social Conflict. *204 pp.*
Dickie-Clark, H. F. Marginal Situation: *A Sociological Study of a Coloured Group. 240 pp. 11 tables.*
Giner, S. and **Archer, M. S.** (Eds.). Contemporary Europe. *Social Structures and Cultural Patterns. 336 pp.*
● **Glaser, Barney** and **Strauss, Anselm L.** Status Passage. *A Formal Theory. 212 pp.*
Glass, D. V. (Ed.) Social Mobility in Britain. *Contributions by J. Berent, T. Bottomore, R. C. Chambers, J. Floud, D. V. Glass, J. R. Hall, H. T. Himmelweit, R. K. Kelsall, F. M. Martin, C. A. Moser, R. Mukherjee, and W. Ziegel. 420 pp.*
Kelsall, R. K. Higher Civil Servants in Britain: *From 1870 to the Present Day. 268 pp. 31 tables.*
● **Lawton, Denis.** Social Class, Language and Education. *192 pp.*
McLeish, John. The Theory of Social Change: *Four Views Considered. 128 pp.*
● **Marsh, David C.** The Changing Social Structure of England and Wales, 1871-1961. *Revised edition. 288 pp.*
Menzies, Ken. Talcott Parsons and the Social Image of Man. *About 208 pp.*
● **Mouzelis, Nicos.** Organization and Bureaucracy. *An Analysis of Modern Theories. 240 pp.*
Ossowski, Stanislaw. Class Structure in the Social Consciousness. *210 pp.*
● **Podgórecki, Adam.** Law and Society. *302 pp.*
Renner, Karl. Institutions of Private Law and Their Social Functions. *Edited, with an Introduction and Notes, by O. Kahn-Freud. Translated by Agnes Schwarzschild. 316 pp.*

Rex, J. and **Tomlinson, S.** Colonial Immigrants in a British City. *A Class Analysis. 368 pp.*
Smooha, S. Israel: Pluralism and Conflict. *472 pp.*
Wesolowski, W. Class, Strata and Power. *Trans. and with Introduction by G. Kolankiewicz. 160 pp.*
Zureik, E. Palestinians in Israel. *A Study in Internal Colonialism. 264 pp.*

SOCIOLOGY AND POLITICS

Acton, T. A. Gypsy Politics and Social Change. *316 pp.*
Burton, F. Politics of Legitimacy. *Struggles in a Belfast Community. 250 pp.*
Etzioni-Halevy, E. Political Manipulation and Administrative Power. *A Comparative Study. About 200 pp.*
●**Hechter, Michael.** Internal Colonialism. *The Celtic Fringe in British National Development, 1536–1966. 380 pp.*
Kornhauser, William. The Politics of Mass Society. *272 pp. 20 tables.*
Korpi, W. The Working Class in Welfare Capitalism. *Work, Unions and Politics in Sweden. 472 pp.*
Kroes, R. Soldiers and Students. *A Study of Right- and Left-wing Students. 174 pp.*
Martin, Roderick. Sociology of Power. *About 272 pp.*
Myrdal, Gunnar. The Political Element in the Development of Economic Theory. *Translated from the German by Paul Streeten. 282 pp.*
Wong, S.-L. Sociology and Socialism in Contemporary China. *160 pp.*
Wootton, Graham. Workers, Unions and the State. *188 pp.*

CRIMINOLOGY

Ancel, Marc. Social Defence: *A Modern Approach to Criminal Problems. Foreword by Leon Radzinowicz. 240 pp.*
Athens, L. Violent Criminal Acts and Actors. *About 150 pp.*
Cain, Maureen E. Society and the Policeman's Role. *326 pp.*
Cloward, Richard A. and **Ohlin, Lloyd E.** Delinquency and Opportunity: *A Theory of Delinquent Gangs. 248 pp.*
Downes, David M. The Delinquent Solution. *A Study in Subcultural Theory. 296 pp.*
Friedlander, Kate. The Psycho-Analytical Approach to Juvenile Delinquency: *Theory, Case Studies, Treatment. 320 pp.*
Gleuck, Sheldon and **Eleanor.** Family Environment and Delinquency. *With the statistical assistance of Rose W. Kneznek. 340 pp.*
Lopez-Rey, Manuel. Crime. *An Analytical Appraisal. 288 pp.*
Mannheim, Hermann. Comparative Criminology: *a Text Book. Two volumes. 442 pp. and 380 pp.*
Morris, Terence. The Criminal Area: *A Study in Social Ecology. Foreword by Hermann Mannheim. 232 pp. 25 tables. 4 maps.*
Podgorecki, A. and **Łos, M.** Multidimensional Sociology. *About 380 pp.*
Rock, Paul. Making People Pay. *338 pp.*

● Taylor, Ian, Walton, Paul, and Young, Jock. The New Criminology. *For a Social Theory of Deviance. 325 pp.*
● Taylor, Ian, Walton, Paul and Young, Jock. (Eds) Critical Criminology. *268 pp.*

SOCIAL PSYCHOLOGY

Bagley, Christopher. The Social Psychology of the Epileptic Child. *320 pp.*

Brittan, Arthur. Meanings and Situations. *224 pp.*

Carroll, J. Break-Out from the Crystal Palace. *200 pp.*

● Fleming, C. M. Adolescence: Its Social Psychology. *With an Introduction to recent findings from the fields of Anthropology, Physiology, Medicine, Psychometrics and Sociometry. 288 pp.*

● The Social Psychology of Education: *An Introduction and Guide to Its Study. 136 pp.*

Linton, Ralph. The Cultural Background of Personality. *132 pp.*

● Mayo, Elton. The Social Problems of an Industrial Civilization. *With an Appendix on the Political Problem. 180 pp.*

Ottaway, A. K. C. Learning Through Group Experience. *176 pp.*

Plummer, Ken. Sexual Stigma. *An Interactionist Account. 254 pp.*

● Rose, Arnold M. (Ed.) Human Behaviour and Social Processes: *an Interactionist Approach. Contributions by Arnold M. Rose, Ralph H. Turner, Anselm Strauss, Everett C. Hughes, E. Franklin Frazier, Howard S. Becker et al. 696 pp.*

Smelser, Neil J. Theory of Collective Behaviour. *448 pp.*

Stephenson, Geoffrey M. The Development of Conscience. *128 pp.*

Young, Kimball. Handbook of Social Psychology. *658 pp. 16 figures. 10 tables.*

SOCIOLOGY OF THE FAMILY

Bell, Colin R. Middle Class Families: *Social and Geographical Mobility. 224 pp.*

Burton, Lindy. Vulnerable Children. *272 pp.*

Gavron, Hannah. The Captive Wife: *Conflicts of Household Mothers. 190 pp.*

George, Victor and Wilding, Paul. Motherless Families. *248 pp.*

Klein, Josephine. Samples from English Cultures.
 1. Three Preliminary Studies and Aspects of Adult Life in England. *447 pp.*
 2. Child-Rearing Practices and Index. *247 pp.*

Klein, Viola. The Feminine Character. *History of an Ideology. 244 pp.*

McWhinnie, Alexina M. Adopted Children. *How They Grow Up. 304 pp.*

● Morgan, D. H. J. Social Theory and the Family. *About 320 pp.*

● Myrdal, Alva and Klein, Viola. Women's Two Roles: *Home and Work. 238 pp. 27 tables.*

Parsons, Talcott and **Bales, Robert F.** Family: Socialization and Interaction Process. *In collaboration with James Olds, Morris Zelditch
and Philip E. Slater. 456 pp. 50 figures and tables.*

SOCIAL SERVICES

Bastide, Roger. The Sociology of Mental Disorder. *Translated from the
French by Jean McNeil. 260 pp.*

Carlebach, Julius. Caring For Children in Trouble. *266 pp.*

George, Victor. Foster Care. *Theory and Practice. 234 pp.*
Social Security: *Beveridge and After. 258 pp.*

George, V. and **Wilding, P.** Motherless Families. *248 pp.*

● **Goetschius, George W.** Working with Community Groups. *256 pp.*

Goetschius, George W. and **Tash, Joan.** Working with Unattached
Youth. *416 pp.*

Heywood, Jean S. Children in Care. *The Development of the Service for
the Deprived Child. Third revised edition. 284 pp.*

King, Roy D., Ranes, Norma V. and **Tizard, Jack.** Patterns of Residen-
tial Care. *356 pp.*

Leigh, John. Young People and Leisure. *256 pp.*

● **Mays, John.** (Ed.) Penelope Hall's Social Services of England and Wales.
About 324 pp.

Morris, Mary. Voluntary Work and the Welfare State. *300 pp.*

Nokes, P. L. The Professional Task in Welfare Practice. *152 pp.*

Timms, Noel. Psychiatric Social Work in Great Britain (1939-1962).
280 pp.

● Social Casework: *Principles and Practice. 256 pp.*

SOCIOLOGY OF EDUCATION

Banks, Olive. Parity and Prestige in English Secondary Education: a
Study in Educational Sociology. *272 pp.*

● **Blyth, W. A. L.** English Primary Education. *A Sociological Description.
2. Background. 168 pp.*

Collier, K. G. The Social Purposes of Education: *Personal and Social
Values in Education. 268 pp.*

Evans, K. M. Sociometry and Education. *158 pp.*

● **Ford, Julienne.** Social Class and the Comprehensive School. *192 pp.*

Foster, P. J. Education and Social Change in Ghana. *336 pp. 3 maps.*

Fraser, W. R. Education and Society in Modern France. *150 pp.*

Grace, Gerald R. Role Conflict and the Teacher. *150 pp.*

Hans, Nicholas. New Trends in Education in the Eighteenth Century.
278 pp. 19 tables.

● Comparative Education: *A Study of Educational Factors and Tra-
ditions. 360 pp.*

● **Hargreaves, David.** Interpersonal Relations and Education. *432 pp.*

● Social Relations in a Secondary School. *240 pp.*

School Organization and Pupil Involvement. *A Study of Secondary
Schools.*

● **Mannheim, Karl** and **Stewart, W.A.C.** An Introduction to the Sociology of Education. *206 pp.*
● Musgrove, F. Youth and the Social Order. *176 pp.*
● **Ottaway, A. K. C.** Education and Society: An Introduction to the Sociology of Education. *With an Introduction by W. O. Lester Smith. 212 pp.*
   Peers, Robert. Adult Education: *A Comparative Study. Revised edition. 398 pp.*
   Stratta, Erica. The Education of Borstal Boys. *A Study of their Educational Experiences prior to, and during, Borstal Training. 256 pp.*
● **Taylor, P. H., Reid, W. A.** and **Holley, B. J.** The English Sixth Form. *A Case Study in Curriculum Research. 198 pp.*

SOCIOLOGY OF CULTURE

   Eppel, E. M. and **M.** Adolescents and Morality: *A Study of some Moral Values and Dilemmas of Working Adolescents in the Context of a changing Climate of Opinion. Foreword by W. J. H. Sprott. 268 pp. 39 tables.*
● **Fromm, Erich.** The Fear of Freedom. *286 pp.*
●   The Sane Society. *400 pp.*
   Johnson, L. The Cultural Critics. *From Matthew Arnold to Raymond Williams. 233 pp.*
   Mannheim, Karl. Essays on the Sociology of Culture. *Edited by Ernst Mannheim in co-operation with Paul Kecskemeti. Editorial Note by Adolph Lowe. 280 pp.*
   Zijderfeld, A. C. On Clichés. *The Supersedure of Meaning by Function in Modernity. About 132 pp.*

SOCIOLOGY OF RELIGION

   Argyle, Michael and **Beit-Hallahmi, Benjamin.** The Social Psychology of Religion. *About 256 pp.*
   Glasner, Peter E. The Sociology of Secularisation. *A Critique of a Concept. About 180 pp.*
   Hall, J. R. The Ways Out. *Utopian Communal Groups in an Age of Babylon. 280 pp.*
   Ranson, S., Hinings, B. and **Bryman, A.** Clergy, Ministers and Priests. *216 pp.*
   Stark, Werner. The Sociology of Religion. *A Study of Christendom.*
     Volume II. *Sectarian Religion. 368 pp.*
     Volume III. *The Universal Church. 464 pp.*
     Volume IV. *Types of Religious Man. 352 pp.*
     Volume V. *Types of Religious Culture. 464 pp.*
   Turner, B. S. Weber and Islam. *216 pp.*
   Watt, W. Montgomery. Islam and the Integration of Society. *320 pp.*

SOCIOLOGY OF ART AND LITERATURE

Jarvie, Ian C. Towards a Sociology of the Cinema. *A Comparative Essay on the Structure and Functioning of a Major Entertainment Industry. 405 pp.*

Rust, Frances S. Dance in Society. *An Analysis of the Relationships between the Social Dance and Society in England from the Middle Ages to the Present Day. 256 pp. 8 pp. of plates.*

Schücking, L. L. The Sociology of Literary Taste. *112 pp.*

Wolff, Janet. Hermeneutic Philosophy and the Sociology of Art. *150 pp.*

SOCIOLOGY OF KNOWLEDGE

Diesing, P. Patterns of Discovery in the Social Sciences. *262 pp.*

● **Douglas, J. D.** (Ed.) Understanding Everyday Life. *370 pp.*

Glasner, B. Essential Interactionism. *About 220 pp.*

● **Hamilton, P.** Knowledge and Social Structure. *174 pp.*

Jarvie, I. C. Concepts and Society. *232 pp.*

Mannheim, Karl. Essays on the Sociology of Knowledge. *Edited by Paul Kecskemeti. Editorial Note by Adolph Lowe. 353 pp.*

Remmling, Gunter W. The Sociology of Karl Mannheim. *With a Bibliographical Guide to the Sociology of Knowledge, Ideological Analysis, and Social Planning. 255 pp.*

Remmling, Gunter W. (Ed.) Towards the Sociology of Knowledge. *Origin and Development of a Sociological Thought Style. 463 pp.*

URBAN SOCIOLOGY

Aldridge, M. The British New Towns. *A Programme Without a Policy. About 250 pp.*

Ashworth, William. The Genesis of Modern British Town Planning: *A Study in Economic and Social History of the Nineteenth and Twentieth Centuries. 288 pp.*

Brittan, A. The Privatised World. *196 pp.*

Cullingworth, J. B. Housing Needs and Planning Policy: *A Restatement of the Problems of Housing Need and 'Overspill' in England and Wales. 232 pp. 44 tables. 8 maps.*

Dickinson, Robert E. City and Region: *A Geographical Interpretation. 608 pp. 125 figures.*

The West European City: *A Geographical Interpretation. 600 pp. 129 maps. 29 plates.*

Humphreys, Alexander J. New Dubliners: *Urbanization and the Irish Family. Foreword by George C. Homans. 304 pp.*

Jackson, Brian. Working Class Community: *Some General Notions raised by a Series of Studies in Northern England. 192 pp.*

● **Mann, P. H.** An Approach to Urban Sociology. *240 pp.*

Mellor, J. R. Urban Sociology in an Urbanized Society. *326 pp.*

Morris, R. N. and **Mogey, J.** The Sociology of Housing. *Studies at Berinsfield. 232 pp. 4 pp. plates.*

Rosser, C. and **Harris, C.** The Family and Social Change. *A Study of Family and Kinship in a South Wales Town. 352 pp. 8 maps.*

● **Stacey, Margaret, Batsone, Eric, Bell, Colin** and **Thurcott, Anne.** Power, Persistence and Change. *A Second Study of Banbury. 196 pp.*

RURAL SOCIOLOGY

Mayer, Adrian C. Peasants in the Pacific. *A Study of Fiji Indian Rural Society. 248 pp. 20 plates.*

Williams, W. M. The Sociology of an English Village: *Gosforth. 272 pp. 12 figures. 13 tables.*

SOCIOLOGY OF INDUSTRY AND DISTRIBUTION

Dunkerley, David. The Foreman. *Aspects of Task and Structure. 192 pp.*

Eldridge, J. E. T. Industrial Disputes. *Essays in the Sociology of Industrial Relations. 288 pp.*

Hollowell, Peter G. The Lorry Driver. *272 pp.*

● **Oxaal, I., Barnett, T.** and **Booth, D.** (Eds) Beyond the Sociology of Development. *Economy and Society in Latin America and Africa. 295 pp.*

Smelser, Neil J. Social Change in the Industrial Revolution: *An Application of Theory to the Lancashire Cotton Industry, 1770–1840. 468 pp. 12 figures. 14 tables.*

Watson, T. J. The Personnel Managers. *A Study in the Sociology of Work and Employment. 262 pp.*

ANTHROPOLOGY

Brandel-Syrier, Mia. Reeftown Elite. *A Study of Social Mobility in a Modern African Community on the Reef. 376 pp.*

Dickie-Clark, H. F. The Marginal Situation. *A Sociological Study of a Coloured Group. 236 pp.*

Dube, S. C. Indian Village. *Foreword by Morris Edward Opler. 276 pp. 4 plates.*

India's Changing Villages: *Human Factors in Community Development. 260 pp. 8 plates. 1 map.*

Firth, Raymond. Malay Fishermen. *Their Peasant Economy. 420 pp. 17 pp. plates.*

Gulliver, P. H. Social Control in an African Society: a Study of the Arusha, Agricultural Masai of Northern Tanganyika. *320 pp. 8 plates. 10 figures.*

Family Herds. *288 pp.*

Jarvie, Ian C. The Revolution in Anthropology. *268 pp.*

Little, Kenneth L. Mende of Sierra Leone. *308 pp. and folder.*

Negroes in Britain. *With a New Introduction and Contemporary Study by Leonard Bloom. 320 pp.*

Madan, G. R. Western Sociologists on Indian Society. *Marx, Spencer, Weber, Durkheim, Pareto. 384 pp.*

Mayer, A. C. Peasants in the Pacific. *A Study of Fiji Indian Rural Society. 248 pp.*

Meer, Fatima. Race and Suicide in South Africa. *325 pp.*

Smith, Raymond T. The Negro Family in British Guiana: *Family Structure and Social Status in the Villages. With a Foreword by Meyer Fortes. 314 pp. 8 plates. 1 figure. 4 maps.*

SOCIOLOGY AND PHILOSOPHY

Barnsley, John H. The Social Reality of Ethics. *A Comparative Analysis of Moral Codes. 448 pp.*

Diesing, Paul. Patterns of Discovery in the Social Sciences. *362 pp.*

● **Douglas, Jack D.** (Ed.) Understanding Everyday Life. *Toward the Reconstruction of Sociological Knowledge. Contributions by Alan F. Blum, Aaron W. Cicourel, Norman K. Denzin, Jack D. Douglas, John Heeren, Peter McHugh, Peter K. Manning, Melvin Power, Matthew Speier, Roy Turner, D. Lawrence Wieder, Thomas P. Wilson and Don H. Zimmerman. 370 pp.*

Gorman, Robert A. The Dual Vision. *Alfred Schutz and the Myth of Phenomenological Social Science. About 300 pp.*

Jarvie, Ian C. Concepts and Society. *216 pp.*

Kilminster, R. Praxis and Method. *A Sociological Dialogue with Lukács, Gramsci and the early Frankfurt School. About 304 pp.*

● **Pelz, Werner.** The Scope of Understanding in Sociology. *Towards a More Radical Reorientation in the Social Humanistic Sciences. 283 pp.*

Roche, Maurice. Phenomenology, Language and the Social Sciences. *371 pp.*

Sahay, Arun. Sociological Analysis. *212 pp.*

Slater, P. Origin and Significance of the Frankfurt School. *A Marxist Perspective. About 192 pp.*

Spurling, L. Phenomenology and the Social World. *The Philosophy of Merleau-Ponty and its Relation to the Social Sciences. 222 pp.*

Wilson, H. T. The American Ideology. *Science, Technology and Organization as Modes of Rationality. 368 pp.*

International Library of Anthropology

General Editor Adam Kuper

Ahmed, A. S. Millenium and Charisma Among Pathans. *A Critical Essay in Social Anthropology. 192 pp.*
Pukhtun Economy and Society. *About 360 pp.*

Brown, Paula. The Chimbu. *A Study of Change in the New Guinea Highlands. 151 pp.*

Foner, N. Jamaica Farewell. *200 pp.*

Gudeman, Stephen. Relationships, Residence and the Individual. *A Rural Panamanian Community. 288 pp. 11 plates, 5 figures, 2 maps, 10 tables.*

    The Demise of a Rural Economy. *From Subsistence to Capitalism in a Latin American Village. 160 pp.*

Hamnett, Ian. Chieftainship and Legitimacy. *An Anthropological Study of Executive Law in Lesotho. 163 pp.*

Hanson, F. Allan. Meaning in Culture. *127 pp.*

Humphreys, S. C. Anthropology and the Greeks. *288 pp.*

Karp, I. Fields of Change Among the Iteso of Kenya. *140 pp.*

Lloyd, P. C. Power and Independence. *Urban Africans' Perception of Social Inequality. 264 pp.*

Parry, J. P. Caste and Kinship in Kangra. *352 pp. Illustrated.*

Pettigrew, Joyce. Robber Noblemen. *A Study of the Political System of the Sikh Jats. 284 pp.*

Street, Brian V. The Savage in Literature. *Representations of 'Primitive' Society in English Fiction, 1858–1920. 207 pp.*

Van Den Berghe, Pierre L. Power and Privilege at an African University. *278 pp.*

International Library of Social Policy

General Editor Kathleen Jones

Bayley, M. Mental Handicap and Community Care. *426 pp.*

Bottoms, A. E. and **McClean, J. D.** Defendants in the Criminal Process. *284 pp.*

Butler, J. R. Family Doctors and Public Policy. *208 pp.*

Davies, Martin. Prisoners of Society. *Attitudes and Aftercare. 204 pp.*

Gittus, Elizabeth. Flats, Families and the Under-Fives. *285 pp.*

Holman, Robert. Trading in Children. *A Study of Private Fostering. 355 pp.*

Jeffs, A. Young People and the Youth Service. *About 180 pp.*

Jones, Howard, and **Cornes, Paul.** Open Prisons. *288 pp.*

Jones, Kathleen. History of the Mental Health Service. *428 pp.*

Jones, Kathleen, with **Brown, John, Cunningham, W. J., Roberts, Julian** and **Williams, Peter.** Opening the Door. *A Study of New Policies for the Mentally Handicapped. 278 pp.*

Karn, Valerie. Retiring to the Seaside. *About 280 pp. 2 maps. Numerous tables.*

King, R. D. and **Elliot, K. W.** Albany: Birth of a Prison—End of an Era. *394 pp.*

Thomas, J. E. The English Prison Officer since 1850: *A Study in Conflict.* *258 pp.*

Walton, R. G. Women in Social Work. *303 pp.*

● **Woodward, J.** To Do the Sick No Harm. *A Study of the British Voluntary Hospital System to 1875. 234 pp.*

International Library of Welfare and Philosophy

General Editors Noel Timms and David Watson

● **McDermott, F. E.** (Ed.) Self-Determination in Social Work. *A Collection of Essays on Self-determination and Related Concepts by Philosophers and Social Work Theorists. Contributors: F. B. Biestek, S. Bernstein, A. Keith-Lucas, D. Sayer, H. H. Perelman, C. Whittington, R. F. Stalley, F. E. McDermott, I. Berlin, H. J. McCloskey, H. L. A. Hart, J. Wilson, A. I. Melden, S. I. Benn. 254 pp.*

● **Plant, Raymond.** Community and Ideology. *104 pp.*

Ragg, Nicholas M. People Not Cases. *A Philosophical Approach to Social Work. About 250 pp.*

● **Timms, Noel** and **Watson, David.** (Eds) Talking About Welfare. *Readings in Philosophy and Social Policy. Contributors: T. H. Marshall, R. B. Brandt, G. H. von Wright, K. Nielsen, M. Cranston, R. M. Titmuss, R. S. Downie, E. Telfer, D. Donnison, J. Benson, P. Leonard, A. Keith-Lucas, D. Walsh, I. T. Ramsey. 320 pp.*

● (Eds). Philosophy in Social Work. *250 pp.*

● **Weale, A.** Equality and Social Policy. *164 pp.*

Primary Socialization, Language and Education

General Editor Basil Bernstein

Adlam, Diana S., *with the assistance of Geoffrey Turner and Lesley Lineker.* Code in Context. *About 272 pp.*

Bernstein, Basil. Class, Codes and Control. *3 volumes.*

● 1. *Theoretical Studies Towards a Sociology of Language. 254 pp.*

2. *Applied Studies Towards a Sociology of Language. 377 pp.*

● 3. *Towards a Theory of Educational Transmission. 167 pp.*

Brandis, W. and **Bernstein, B.** Selection and Control. *176 pp.*

Brandis, Walter and **Henderson, Dorothy.** Social Class, Language and Communication. *288 pp.*

Cook-Gumperz, Jenny. Social Control and Socialization. *A Study of Class Differences in the Language of Maternal Control. 290 pp.*

● **Gahagan, D. M** and **G. A.** Talk Reform. *Exploration in Language for Infant School Children. 160 pp.*

Hawkins, P. R. Social Class, the Nominal Group and Verbal Strategies. *About 220 pp.*

Robinson, W. P. and **Rackstraw, Susan D. A.** A Question of Answers. *2 volumes. 192 pp. and 180 pp.*

Turner, Geoffrey J. and **Mohan, Bernard A.** A Linguistic Description and Computer Programme for Children's Speech. *208 pp.*

Reports of the Institute of Community Studies

Baker, J. The Neighbourhood Advice Centre. A Community Project in Camden. *320 pp.*

● **Cartwright, Ann.** Patients and their Doctors. *A Study of General Practice. 304 pp.*

Dench, Geoff. Maltese in London. *A Case-study in the Erosion of Ethnic Consciousness. 302 pp.*

Jackson, Brian and **Marsden, Dennis.** Education and the Working Class: *Some General Themes raised by a Study of 88 Working-class Children in a Northern Industrial City. 268 pp. 2 folders.*

Marris, Peter. The Experience of Higher Education. *232 pp. 27 tables.*

● Loss and Change. *192 pp.*

Marris, Peter and **Rein, Martin.** Dilemmas of Social Reform. *Poverty and Community Action in the United States. 256 pp.*

Marris, Peter and **Somerset, Anthony.** African Businessmen. *A Study of Entrepreneurship and Development in Keyna. 256 pp.*

Mills, Richard. Young Outsiders: *a Study in Alternative Communities. 216 pp.*

Runciman, W. G. Relative Deprivation and Social Justice. *A Study of Attitudes to Social Inequality in Twentieth-Century England. 352 pp.*

Willmott, Peter. Adolescent Boys in East London. *230 pp.*

Willmott, Peter and **Young, Michael.** Family and Class in a London Suburb. *202 pp. 47 tables.*

Young, Michael and **McGeeney, Patrick.** Learning Begins at Home. *A Study of a Junior School and its Parents. 128 pp.*

Young, Michael and **Willmott, Peter.** Family and Kinship in East London. *Foreword by Richard M. Titmuss. 252 pp. 39 tables.*

The Symmetrical Family. *410 pp.*

Reports of the Institute for Social Studies in Medical Care

Cartwright, Ann, Hockey, Lisbeth and **Anderson, John J.** Life Before Death. *310 pp.*

Dunnell, Karen and **Cartwright, Ann.** Medicine Takers, Prescribers and Hoarders. *190 pp.*

Farrell, C. My Mother Said. . . . *A Study of the Way Young People Learned About Sex and Birth Control. 200 pp.*

Medicine, Illness and Society

General Editor W. M. Williams

Hall, David J. Social Relations & Innovation. *Changing the State of Play in Hospitals. 232 pp.*

Hall, David J., and **Stacey, M.** (Eds) Beyond Separation. *234 pp.*

Robinson, David. The Process of Becoming Ill. *142 pp.*

Stacey, Margaret *et al.* Hospitals, Children and Their Families. *The Report of a Pilot Study. 202 pp.*

Stimson G. V. and **Webb, B.** Going to See the Doctor. *The Consultation Process in General Practice. 155 pp.*

Monographs in Social Theory

General Editor Arthur Brittan

● **Barnes, B.** Scientific Knowledge and Sociological Theory. *192 pp.*

Bauman, Zygmunt. Culture as Praxis. *204 pp.*

● **Dixon, Keith.** Sociological Theory. *Pretence and Possibility. 142 pp.*

Meltzer, B. N., Petras, J. W. and **Reynolds, L. T.** Symbolic Interactionism. *Genesis, Varieties and Criticisms. 144 pp.*

● **Smith, Anthony D.** The Concept of Social Change. *A Critique of the Functionalist Theory of Social Change. 208 pp.*

Routledge Social Science Journals

The British Journal of Sociology. *Editor – Angus Stewart; Associate Editor – Leslie Sklair. Vol. 1, No. 1 – March 1950 and Quarterly. Roy. 8vo. All back issues available. An international journal publishing original papers in the field of sociology and related areas.*

Community Work. *Edited by David Jones and Marjorie Mayo. 1973. Published annually.*

Economy and Society. *Vol. 1, No. 1. February 1972 and Quarterly. Metric Roy. 8vo. A journal for all social scientists covering sociology, philosophy, anthropology, economics and history. All back numbers available.*

Ethnic and Racial Studies. *Editor – John Stone. Vol. 1 – 1978. Published quarterly.*

Religion. Journal of Religion and Religions. *Chairman of Editorial Board, Ninian Smart. Vol. 1, No. 1, Spring 1971. A journal with an interdisciplinary approach to the study of the phenomena of religion. All back numbers available.*

Sociology of Health and Illness. *A Journal of Medical Sociology. Editor – Alan Davies; Associate Editor – Ray Jobling. Vol. 1, Spring 1979. Published 3 times per annum.*

Year Book of Social Policy in Britain, The. *Edited by Kathleen Jones. 1971. Published annually.*

Social and Psychological Aspects of Medical Practice

Editor   Trevor Silverstone

Lader, Malcolm. Psychophysiology of Mental Illness. *280 pp.*
● **Silverstone, Trevor** and **Turner, Paul.** Drug Treatment in Psychiatry. *Revised edition. 256 pp.*
Whiteley, J. S. and **Gordon, J.** Group Approaches in Psychiatry. *256 pp.*